UKRAINE 2016 HUMAN RIGHTS REPORT

Note: Except where otherwise noted, references in this report do not include areas controlled by Russian-backed separatist forces in the Donbas region of eastern Ukraine or Russian-occupied Crimea. At the end of this report is a section listing human rights abuses in Russian-occupied Crimea.

EXECUTIVE SUMMARY

Ukraine is a republic with a semi-presidential political system composed of three branches of government: a unicameral legislature (Verkhovna Rada), an executive led by a directly elected president and a prime minister chosen through a legislative majority, and a judiciary. The country held presidential and legislative elections in 2014; international and domestic observers considered both elections free and fair.

Civilian authorities generally maintained effective control over security forces in the territory controlled by the government.

The most significant human rights problems in the country during the year were:

Conflict- and Occupation-related Abuses: Russian-backed separatists in Donbas engaged in abductions, torture, and unlawful detention, employed child soldiers, stifled dissent, and restricted humanitarian aid. To a lesser extent, there were also reports of some of these practices by government forces. In Crimea, Russian occupation authorities systematically targeted perceived dissidents for abuse and politically motivated prosecution.

Corruption and Official Impunity: The country suffered from impunity for corruption and deficiencies in the administration of justice. The Prosecutor General's Office and the judicial system proved largely unable to convict perpetrators of past or current major corruption.

Insufficient Support for Internally Displaced Persons (IDPs): Russia's occupation of Crimea and aggression in eastern Ukraine resulted in 1.7 million IDPs who faced continuing difficulties obtaining legal documents, education, pensions, and access to financial institutions and health care. During the year the government suspended all social payments for IDPs, pending verification of their presence in government-controlled territory, ostensibly to combat fraudulent payments.

Other problems reported during the year included: alleged beatings and torture of detainees and prisoners, as well as harsh conditions in government-run prisons and detention facilities; nongovernmental attacks on journalists; societal violence against women and abuse of children; societal discrimination against and harassment of ethnic and religious minorities; trafficking in persons, including forced labor; discrimination and harassment against lesbian, gay, bisexual, transgender, and intersex (LGBTI) persons; and discrimination against persons with HIV/AIDS. There also were limitations on workers' right to strike, and failure to enforce effectively labor laws and occupational safety and health standards for the workplace.

The government generally failed to take adequate steps to prosecute or punish most officials who committed abuses, resulting in a climate of impunity. Human rights groups and the United Nations noted significant deficiencies in investigations into human rights abuses committed by government security forces, in particular into allegations of torture, enforced disappearances, arbitrary detention, and other abuses reportedly perpetrated by the Security Service of Ukraine (SBU). The perpetrators of the 2014 Euromaidan shootings in Kyiv and riots in Odesa have not been held to account.

Investigations into alleged human rights abuses related to Russia's occupation of Crimea and the continuing aggression in the Donbas region remained incomplete due to lack of government control in those territories and the refusal of Russia and Russian-backed separatists to investigate abuse allegations.

Section 1. Respect for the Integrity of the Person, Including Freedom from:

a. Arbitrary Deprivation of Life and other Unlawful or Politically Motivated Killings

There were several reports that the government or its agents committed arbitrary or unlawful killings.

According to media reports, police in Kryve Ozero allegedly beat a man to death on August 24, after responding to a domestic violence call. Authorities detained four police officers on suspicion of murder. In response, the chief of the National Police disbanded a police station where the killing occurred. On October 2, the detained officers were released on bail; the pretrial investigation continues.

There were also reports of killings by government and Russian-backed separatist forces in connection with the conflict in Luhansk and Donetsk Oblasts (see section 1.g.).

There were reports of politically motivated killings by nongovernment actors.

On July 20, a car bomb in Kyiv killed Belarusian-born journalist, Pavel Sheremet, as he drove in a car belonging to his partner, Olena Prytula. Sheremet, a Russian citizen, worked for *Ukrainska Pravda* newspaper and Vesti radio station, where he had been critical of Ukrainian, Russian, and Belarusian authorities. Authorities released a video of two individuals placing the device under the car. As of year's end, the investigation remained open and authorities had made no arrests.

On March 9, Yuriy Hrabovsky, a lawyer representing a detained Russian special forces soldier, Aleksandr Aleksandrov, disappeared in Odesa. On March 25, his body was found in a shallow roadside grave. The killing remained under investigation at year's end, and authorities had made no arrests.

Human rights organizations and media reported deaths in prisons or detention centers due to torture or negligence by police or prison officers (see section 1.c., Prison and Detention Center Conditions).

Law enforcement agencies continued to investigate killings and other crimes committed during the Euromaidan protests in Kyiv in 2013-14. Human rights groups were critical of the low number of convictions despite considerable evidence. Human rights groups also criticized prosecutors for focusing on low-ranking officials while taking little action to investigate government leaders believed to have been involved. According to the Prosecutor General's Office, as of mid-November, courts had convicted 45 persons investigated for Euromaidan-related crimes, 152 were on trial, and 190 remained under investigation.

Law enforcement agencies also continued their investigation into the events in Odesa in 2014 in which 48 persons died, including six government supporters and 42 persons who supported more autonomy for regions. Those who supported autonomy died in a fire at the Trade Union Building; authorities largely failed to investigate these deaths, focusing on alleged crimes committed by individuals seeking more autonomy. A Council of Europe report in 2015 found the government's investigation lacked independence and that the Prosecutor General's Office and the Ministry of Internal Affairs failed to conduct a thorough, coordinated investigation. On January 15, a group of civil society activists and journalists released a statement expressing their lack of confidence in the investigation by the Prosecutor General's Office and the Ministry of Internal Affairs, accusing the authorities of sabotaging the investigation to prevent the perpetrators from being brought to justice. On May 4, Odesa police chief, Petro Lutsiuk, was fired from his position, and the Prosecutor General's Office later charged him with abuse of authority in connection with the events at the trade union building. Court hearings continued through the year's end.

b. Disappearance

There were multiple reports of politically motivated disappearances, particularly in relation to the conflict between the government and combined Russian and separatist forces in the Donbas region and by Russian occupation authorities in Crimea (see section 1.g., Crimea subsection).

c. Torture and Other Cruel, Inhuman, or Degrading Treatment or Punishment

Although the constitution and law prohibit torture and other cruel punishment, there were reports that law enforcement authorities engaged in such abuse. While courts cannot legally use as evidence in court proceedings confessions and statements under duress made to police by persons in custody, there were reports that police and other law enforcement officials abused and, at times, tortured persons in custody to obtain confessions.

In the Donbas region, there were reports that government and progovernment forces engaged in military operations at times committed human rights abuses, including torture. There were reports that Russian-backed separatist forces in the self-proclaimed "people's republics" of Donetsk and Luhansk systematically committed numerous abuses, including torture, to maintain control or for personal financial gain. According to international organizations and nongovernmental organizations (NGOs), abuses included beatings, forced labor, psychological and physical torture, public humiliation, and sexual violence (see section 1.g.).

In a July joint report, Amnesty International (AI) and Human Rights Watch (HRW) highlighted allegations of the use of torture at SBU detention sites, including beatings, starvation, and electric shocks.

In its March report, the UN Human Rights Monitoring Mission in Ukraine (HRMMU), under the Office of the UN High Commissioner for Human Rights, gave an undated account of a "profederalism" activist who was allegedly tortured and pressured to sign a confession at an SBU facility in Odesa. The government asserted that such "profederalist" messaging was used by Russia to weaken Ukraine's central government. The man reported that during interrogation the SBU suffocated him with a plastic bag and beat him. Afterwards, the SBU brought the man to the lobby of the SBU building to witness that authorities had also arrested his son. His son was then brought to a neighboring cell, where the father could hear his son scream as he was abused.

Abuse of prisoners and detainees by police and prison authorities remained a widespread problem. For example, on August 23, 15 staff members of the Chernihiv pretrial detention facility reportedly beat 25-year-old Viktor Kravchenko. After the beating, facility staff placed him in a disciplinary cell and denied his request for medical help. The facility's administration denied any wrongdoing.

There were reports of hazing in the military. On August 4, the country's human rights ombudsman sent a letter to the Prosecutor General's Office and the Ministry of Defense expressing concern about military hazing following the suicide of Vlad Khaisuk, a young soldier serving in a unit stationed in Stanytsia Luhanska. After Khaisuk's suicide, his parents found videos on Khaisuk's smartphone of him being hazed and humiliated by other soldiers. The Luhansk Department of the Military Prosecutor's Office investigated and found no signs of military hazing. At year's end, however, police in Stanytsia Luhanska were investigating the accident as a homicide.

In its September report, the HRMMU noted that it "continued to document cases of sexual violence, amounting to torture, of conflict-related detainees, both men and women. It includes cases of rape, and threats of rape or other forms of sexual violence towards victims and/or their relatives." In one example, the HRMMU described a case in March where unidentified members of the security services detained a man, took him to an abandoned building, and interrogated him about the positions of armed groups. When he could not provide information, the perpetrators chained him to a metal cage, took a ramrod, and inserted it into the man's urethra, causing him severe pain.

During the first nine months of the year, the Prosecutor General's Office forwarded for prosecution 35 cases specifically alleging torture or degrading treatment involving law enforcement officers.

According to the Ministry of Internal Affairs, during the first nine months of the year, authorities opened 133 criminal cases against police officers for crimes including torture, illegal arrests and searches, and illegal confiscation of property. Of these alleged cases of abuse, five were for alleged torture. Authorities imposed disciplinary actions against 20 officers and fired 10.

Prison and Detention Center Conditions

Prison and detention center conditions remained poor, did not meet international standards, and at times posed a serious threat to the life and health of prisoners. Physical abuse, lack of proper medical care and nutrition, poor sanitation, and lack of adequate light were persistent problems. The Ukrainian Helsinki Human Rights Union maintained that life sentences amounted to slow executions of prisoners because of the poor conditions of their imprisonment.

Physical Conditions: Authorities generally held adults and juveniles in separate facilities, although there were reports that juveniles and adults were not separated in some pretrial detention facilities.

Conditions in police temporary detention facilities and State Penitentiary Service pretrial detention facilities were harsher than in low- and medium-security prisons. Despite a reduction in the number of inmates, overcrowding remained a problem in pretrial detention facilities. Temporary detention facilities often lacked adequate sanitation and medical facilities.

Physical abuse by guards was a problem. For example, according to the Ombudsman's Office, the staff of the Kryzhopil Correctional Center Number 113 in Vinnytsia Oblast systematically violated prisoners' rights during the year. Inmates complained to the Ombudsman's Office about illegal actions of the administration, including systematic beatings, forced and unpaid labor, and lack of medical care. The monitoring team found that a convicted person kept in one of the disciplinary cells tried to commit suicide, which he claimed was due to fear of physical violence by the prison administration. The local prosecutor's office launched an investigation into the actions of the correctional facility administration.

There were reports of prisoner-on-prisoner violence. For example, on June 6, an inmate of the Shepetivka correctional facility in Khmelnytskyi Oblast died of a traumatic brain injury inflicted by his fellow inmates. The penitentiary service conducted an investigation of the incident.

According to the Association of Independent Monitors and the Human Rights Ombudsman's Office, authorities failed to protect the lives and human rights of prisoners in areas close to the zone of operation against combined Russian and separatist forces in eastern Ukraine adequately and failed to evacuate staff and inmates in a timely fashion. As of September 1, under the auspices of the Ombudsman's Office, 17 prisoners incarcerated in territories seized by Russian-backed separatist forces were transferred to penal facilities on government-controlled territory.

The condition of prison facilities and places of unofficial detention in areas held by Russian-backed separatist forces was very poor. According to the Justice for Peace coalition, there was an extensive network of unofficial places of detention in the Donetsk and Luhansk Oblasts located in basements, sewage wells, garages, and industrial enterprises. In most cases the places of detention were not suitable for even short-term detention. There were reports of shortages of food, water, heat, sanitation, and proper medical care.

According to October press reports citing information from the Eastern Human Rights Group, abuse of prisoners was widespread in areas not controlled by the government. Prior to the conflict, more than 5,000 prisoners were held in the part of Luhansk Oblast under the control of Russian-backed separatists. According to the group, prison conditions had deteriorated severely. The groups reported systemic abuses, such as torture, starvation, denial of medical care, and solitary confinement, as well as the extensive use of prisoners as slave labor to produce goods that, when sold, provided a direct source of personal income to Russian-backed separatist leaders.

Administration: Authorities kept records of prisoners in detention, but they were occasionally incomplete. In areas controlled by Russian-backed separatist forces, authorities lacked central record keeping, leading to difficulties for prisoners and arbitrarily held detainees. Human rights groups reported instances in which authorities confiscated prisoners' identification cards and failed to return them upon their release. Prisoners released by Russian-backed separatists often had no identification. There was no prison ombudsman.

In government-controlled areas, prisoners could file complaints with the Office of the Parliamentary Ombudsman for Human Rights. As of October 1, the ombudsman's office received 1,114 complaints from prisoners and their relatives throughout the country. The most common complaints were regarding a lack of appropriate living and sanitary conditions; cruel, inhuman, and degrading treatment; public humiliation; limited communication with family members and relatives; unjustified punishment; denial of the right to legal consultation; and denial of the right to submit a complaint about actions of the administration. Prisoners also complained about inadequate medical treatment and precautions. For example, authorities did not isolate prisoners with contagious tuberculosis from other patients.

Although prisoners and detainees may file complaints about conditions in custody with the human rights ombudsman, human rights organizations noted prison officials continued to censor or discourage complaints and penalized and abused inmates who filed them. Rights groups reported that legal norms did not always provide for confidentiality of complaints.

Officials generally allowed prisoners to receive visitors, with the exception of those in disciplinary cells. Prisoner rights groups noted some families had to pay bribes to obtain permission for prison visits to which they are entitled by law.

Independent Monitoring: The government generally permitted independent monitoring of prisons and detention centers by international and local human rights groups. On May 25, the UN Subcommittee on the Prevention of Torture (SPT) suspended its visit to the country after being denied access to places in several parts of the country where it suspected the SBU was illegally depriving individuals of their liberty. On September 5, the SPT resumed its visit and was granted access to the facilities. During the year the Ombudsperson's Office together with representatives of civil society conducted monitoring visits to penitentiary facilities in 15 oblasts.

d. Arbitrary Arrest or Detention

The constitution and law prohibit arbitrary arrest and detention, but serious problems remained.

AI and HRW reported details of arbitrary secret detentions by the SBU that emerged following the release of 13 persons from an SBU facility in Kharkiv (see section 1.b.). One of those detained, Viktor Ashykhin, was kidnapped from his hometown of Ukrainsk in 2014 and released in July. He told AI that he was moved three times during his 597-day illegal detention to hide him from independent monitors.

The HRMMU, AI, HRW, and other international groups reported numerous unauthorized detentions in areas of Donbas controlled by Russian-backed separatists (see section 1.g.).

Role of the Police and Security Apparatus

The Ministry of Internal Affairs is responsible for maintaining internal security and order. The ministry oversees police and other law enforcement personnel. The SBU is responsible for all state security, nonmilitary intelligence, and counterintelligence matters. The Ministry of Internal Affairs reports to the Cabinet of Ministers, and the SBU reports directly to the president. The State Fiscal Service exercises law enforcement powers through the tax police and reports to the Cabinet of Ministers. The State Migration Service under the Ministry of Internal Affairs implements state policy regarding border security, migration, citizenship, and registration of refugees and other migrants.

Civilian authorities generally had control over law enforcement agencies but rarely took action to punish abuses committed by security forces.

Impunity for abuses by law enforcement remained a significant problem frequently highlighted by the HRMMU in its reports and by other human rights groups. In its September report, the HRMMU attributed the problem to "pressure on the judiciary, [and] inability and unwillingness of the Office of the Prosecutor General and Office of the Military Prosecutor to investigate" abuses. The HRMMU also noted that authorities were unwilling to investigate allegations of torture, particularly when victims were detained on grounds related to national security or were seen as proseparatist.

While authorities sometimes brought charges against members of the security services, cases often remained under investigation without being brought to trial, while authorities allowed alleged perpetrators to continue their work. Additionally, human rights groups criticized the lack of progress in investigations of alleged crimes in areas retaken by Ukraine from Russian-backed separatists, resulting in continuing impunity for these crimes. In particular, investigations of alleged crimes committed by Russian-backed separatist forces in Slovyansk and Kramatorsk in 2014 appeared stalled. Human rights groups believed that many of the local law enforcement personnel in both cities collaborated with Russian-backed separatists when they controlled these cities.

Under the law members of the Verkhovna Rada have authority to conduct investigations and public hearings into law enforcement problems. The human rights ombudsman may also initiate investigations into abuses by security forces.

Security forces generally prevented or responded to societal violence. At times, however, they used excessive force to disperse protests and, in some cases, failed to protect victims from harassment or violence. For example, on September 1, approximately 100 persons attacked a camp of peaceful demonstrators near the Odesa City Council on Dumska Street. The attackers pushed protesters from the square using fire extinguishers and tear gas and destroyed their camp. A few protesters were injured and hospitalized. According to witnesses, police watched and did nothing to prevent the clashes.

Arrest Procedures and Treatment of Detainees

By law authorities may detain a suspect for three days without a warrant, after which time a judge must issue a warrant authorizing continued detention. Authorities in some cases detained persons for longer than three days without a warrant.

Prosecutors must bring detainees before a judge within 72 hours, and pretrial detention should not exceed six months for minor crimes and 12 months for serious ones. Persons have the right to consult a lawyer upon their detention. According to the law, prosecutors may detain suspects accused of terrorist activities for up to 30 days without charges or a bench warrant. Under the law citizens have the right to be informed of the charges brought against them. Authorities must promptly inform detainees of their rights and immediately notify family members of an arrest. Police often did not follow these procedures. Police at times failed to keep records or register detained suspects, and courts often extended detention to allow police more time to obtain confessions. Authorities kept suspects under house arrest and occasionally held them incommunicado, in some instances for several weeks.

Under the law the government must provide attorneys for indigent defendants. Compliance was inconsistent because of a shortage of defense attorneys or because attorneys, citing low government compensation, refused to defend indigent clients. According to the Ministry of Justice, 60,500 persons received free legal aid. As of September 1, there were 550 points of access to free legal aid throughout the government-controlled areas of the country.

The law provides for bail, but many defendants could not pay the required amounts. Courts sometimes imposed travel restrictions as an alternative to pretrial confinement. Under the criminal procedure code, prosecutors need a court order to impose travel restrictions on persons awaiting trial. Prosecutors must prove the restrictions are the minimum needed to ensure that suspects will appear at hearings and not interfere with criminal proceedings.

Arbitrary Arrest: The HRMMU reported a pattern of arbitrary detention by authorities. In its September report, the HRMMU reported that the SBU apprehended a married couple in Odesa and reportedly held the couple incommunicado at an SBU compound for 20 hours before recording their detention. SBU also reportedly subjected them to threats, sleep deprivation, interrogation without a lawyer present, and denied requests for legal counsel.

The HRMMU expressed concern over mass arrests in government-controlled portions of Donetsk and Luhansk Oblasts. These oblasts are subject to the Law on Combatting Terrorism, which allows authorities to make arrests with a lower standard of proof than allowed under the criminal procedure code, leading in some cases to arbitrary arrest. For example, in its March report, the HRMMU cited SBU raids, conducted in December 2015 in Krasnohorivka and Avdiivka in Donetsk oblast, in which authorities detained hundreds of persons for several hours for questioning about alleged affiliation with armed groups. Authorities subsequently released most detainees.

Detainee's Ability to Challenge Lawfulness of Detention before a Court: Under the law citizens have the right to challenge an arrest in court or by appeal to a prosecutor to obtain prompt release in cases of unlawful detention.

Protracted Detention of Rejected Asylum Seekers or Stateless Persons: Authorities frequently detained asylum seekers for extended periods without court approval. They also regularly detained asylum seekers prior to their deportation (see section 2.d.).

e. Denial of Fair Public Trial

While the constitution provides for an independent judiciary and the Verkhovna Rada passed a judicial reform package in June, courts were inefficient and remained vulnerable to political pressure and corruption. Confidence in the judiciary remained low.

On June 2, parliament adopted amendments to the constitution regarding the judiciary. The amendments give new powers to the High Council of Justice, stipulate that the majority of High Council members must be judges, and authorize the High Council to make decisions on the election, dismissal, transfer, promotion, and immunity of judges. Parliament and the president no longer have decisive roles in these processes, which limit potential interference with the judiciary. Certain provisions will be implemented gradually. For example, the president retains the right to decide on the transfer of judges for two years.

On September 30, the Law on Judiciary and Status of Judges came into effect, facilitating the implementation of the above constitutional amendments. The law introduces a three-tier system of courts, with the Supreme Court as the highest judicial body, holding the authority to rescind lower courts' judgments. The law provides for wider civil society engagement in the selection and assessment of judges through a new consultative body called the Public Integrity Council. The law allows anyone to initiate disciplinary proceedings against a judge before the High Council of Justice and imposes anticorruption measures on judges.

As of October 1, the Prosecutor General's Office had brought 16 criminal cases against judges to court.

Judges continued to complain about weak separation of powers between the executive and judicial branches of government. Some judges claimed that high-ranking politicians pressured them to decide cases in their favor, regardless of the merits. Other factors impeded the right to a fair trial, such as lengthy court proceedings, particularly in administrative courts, inadequate funding, and the inability of courts to enforce rulings. According to the human rights ombudsman, authorities fully executed only 40 percent of court rulings.

There were reports of intimidation and attacks against lawyers representing defendants considered "pro-Russian" or "proseparatist." For example, on January 26 in Kharkiv, an unoccupied car belonging to lawyer Oleksandr Shadrin exploded. Shadrin had been working on a number of high-profile cases involving "proseparatist" defendants. On January 29, the Ukrainian Bar Association issued an open letter of concern about the incident involving Shadrin's car as well as other cases in which the safety of attorneys was threatened. In a similar incident on February 2 in Kyiv, an unoccupied car belonging to another lawyer, Andriy Fedur, exploded. Fedur had been defending the accused murderers of journalists Oles Buzyna and Heorgiy Gongadze.

Trial Procedures

A single judge decides most cases, although two judges and three public assessors who have some legal training hear trials on charges carrying the maximum sentence of life imprisonment. The law provides for cross-examination of witnesses by both prosecutors and defense attorneys and for plea bargaining.

The law presumes defendants are innocent, and they cannot be legally compelled to testify or confess, although high conviction rates called into question the legal presumption of innocence. Defendants have the right to be informed promptly and in detail of the charges against them, with interpretation as needed; to a public trial without undue delay; to be present at their trial, to communicate privately with an attorney of their choice (or one provided at public expense); and to have adequate time and facilities to prepare a defense. The law also allows defendants access to government-held evidence, to confront witnesses against them, to present witnesses and evidence, and the right to appeal. The law applies to all defendants regardless of ethnicity, gender, or age.

Trials are open to the public, but some judges prohibited media from observing proceedings. While trials must start no later than three weeks after charges are filed, prosecutors seldom met this requirement. Human rights groups reported that officials occasionally monitored meetings between defense attorneys and their clients.

Political Prisoners and Detainees

On May 12, an Ivano-Frankivsk court sentenced blogger Ruslan Kotsaba to three-and-a-half years in prison, on charges that he had impeded the work of the armed forces with his calls to ignore the military draft. Authorities arrested Kotsaba in 2015, and human rights groups deemed him a political prisoner. The court dropped a more serious charge of treason. On July 24, an appeals court overturned the conviction, freeing Kotsaba after 18 months in detention.

Civil Judicial Procedures and Remedies

The constitution and law provide for the right to seek redress for any decisions, actions, or omissions of national and local government officials that violate citizens' human rights. An inefficient and corrupt judicial system limited the right of redress. Individuals may also file a collective legal challenge to legislation they believe may violate basic rights and freedoms. Individuals may appeal to the human rights ombudsman at any time and to the European Court of Human Rights after exhausting domestic legal remedies.

f. Arbitrary or Unlawful Interference with Privacy, Family, Home, or Correspondence

The constitution prohibits such actions, but there were reports authorities generally did not respect the prohibitions.

By law the SBU may not conduct surveillance or searches without a court-issued warrant. In practice, however, law enforcement agencies sometimes conducted searches without a proper warrant. In an emergency authorities may initiate a search without prior court approval, but they must seek court approval immediately after the investigation begins. Citizens have the right to examine any dossier in the possession of the SBU that concerns them; they have the right to recover losses resulting from an investigation. Because there was no implementing legislation, authorities generally did not respect these rights, and many citizens were not aware of their rights or that authorities had violated their privacy.

On October 28, the newspaper *Ukrainska Pravda* published an open appeal to the president and heads of the SBU, the National Police, and the Ministry of Internal Affairs. The appeal concerned recordings the newspaper received from an anonymous source, which indicated that its journalists and editors had been under SBU surveillance at the request of high-level officials in late 2015 and possibly beyond. The newspaper demanded to know why, how, and on whose authority the surveillance had taken place. The official SBU response said that national security legislation prohibited the disclosure of information sought by *Ukrainska Pravda*.

g. Abuses in Internal Conflicts

Russia controls the level of violence in eastern Ukraine, intensifying the conflict when it suits its political interests, while largely ignoring the September 2014 ceasefire and subsequent attempts to reestablish the ceasefire agreed to by all sides. Russia has continued to arm, train, lead, and fight alongside separatists, and Russian-backed separatists have methodically obstructed and threatened international monitors throughout the conflict, who do not have the access necessary to record systematically ceasefire violations or abuses committed by separatist authorities or combined Russian-separatist forces.

International organizations and NGOs, including AI, HRW, and the UN Office of the High Commissioner for Human Rights (UNHCR) issued periodic reports of human rights abuses committed in the Donbas region by combined Russian-separatist and by government forces. As of August 17, the Organization for Security and Cooperation in Europe (OSCE) fielded 1,102 persons supporting a special monitoring mission, which issued daily reports on the situation and conditions in most major cities.

As of September 15, the HRMMU reported that fighting had killed at least 9,578 persons, including civilians, government armed forces, and members of armed groups. This figure included the 298 passengers and crew on board Malaysian Airlines flight MH-17, which was shot down in 2014 over the Donbas region. Additionally, more than three million residents have left areas of Donetsk and Luhansk Oblasts controlled by Russian-backed separatists since the start of the conflict. As of November 15, the Ministry of Social Policy had registered 1.7 million IDPs, although civil society groups believed the actual number to be lower. According to UNHCR there were approximately 1.4 million Ukrainian refugees in other countries, including approximately one million in the Russian Federation.

Media and human rights groups continued to report widespread human rights abuses in areas held by Russian-backed separatist forces. The HRMMU noted a "collapse of law and order" in such areas as well as "serious human rights abuses," including killings and torture.

<u>Killings</u>: A May 4 special HRMMU report on "extrajudicial, summary, or arbitrary executions" occurring in the context of the conflict in eastern Ukraine expressed strong concern about both sides' use of "inherently indiscriminate weapons, such as cluster munitions and landmines." The HRMMU noted in its September report the "widespread practice" by both sides of "engaging in hostilities from residential areas, with civilians suffering the impact of return fire." For example, on August 24, in the government-controlled area of Donetsk Oblast, a woman in the village of Zolote-4 died while lying in bed, when Russian-backed separatist forces fired on the village.

The HRMMU, the OSCE Special Monitoring Mission, and human rights groups did not report any extrajudicial killings by government forces during the year in connection with the conflict. Several cases from previous years remained under investigation.

There were no reports by the HRMMU or human rights organizations of extrajudicial killings of civilians by combined Russian-separatist forces during the year, although the press reported several instances. The HRMMU identified unreported cases of extrajudicial killings from previous years that authorities had not yet investigated.

According to press reports, on July 20, three drunken members of the Russian-backed separatist "7th separate motorized rifle brigade" robbed, then shot and killed a resident of the village of Komsomolsk, Luhansk Oblast. Russian-backed separatist authorities reportedly dismissed the men from their positions to conceal their involvement in the killing.

On February 17, a video appeared on the internet showing a Russian fighter code-named "Olkhon" whipping Donbas resident, Alexei Frumkin, with an electrical cord while Frumkin was tied to a post. The combined Russian and separatist battalion that released the video claimed that "Olkhon" killed Frumkin immediately after the video was shot. According to press reports, Frumkin had supported Russian-backed separatists but had vanished in the autumn of 2014, and his fate had been unknown until the video was released. It is unknown when the video was recorded.

In its June report, the HRMMU noted that "since mid-April 2014, up to 2,000 civilians have been killed in armed hostilities, mostly as a result of indiscriminate shelling of populated areas…. Dozens of individuals were subjected to summary executions and killings, or died of torture and ill-treatment in custody. Hundreds of persons remained missing--either in secret detention or, most likely, killed--with their bodies pending recovery or identification." According to Iryna Herashchenko, Ukrainian representative to the humanitarian subgroup of the Trilateral Contact Group, 498 persons, including 347 civilians, were missing in Donbas in August. Human rights groups criticized the government for not keeping an effective database of missing persons. Russian-backed separatists had no such system and no effective means of investigating missing persons cases. According to human rights groups, approximately 1,000 bodies in government-controlled cemeteries and morgues, both military and civilian, remained unidentified as a result of fighting, mostly from 2014. According to the HRMMU, government authorities lacked coordination among law enforcement bodies in determining the whereabouts of missing persons and the identification of remains.

<u>Abductions</u>: Government forces, Russian-backed-separatist forces, and criminal elements engaged in abductions. The HRMMU noted a pattern of arbitrary and

incommunicado detention by government law enforcement bodies (mainly by the SBU) and by military and paramilitary units, first and foremost by the former volunteer battalions now formally incorporated into the security services.

In its reports, the HRMMU repeatedly expressed concern about reports of enforced disappearances and "unacknowledged detention" practiced by the Security Service of Ukraine (SBU). On July 21, HRW and AI released a report, *You Don't Exist*, which documented nine alleged cases of enforced disappearances by the SBU at alleged secret detention facilities in Kharkiv, Kramatorsk, Izyum, and Mariupol. The report highlighted the case of Konstantin Beskorovayni, a local official from the town of Konstantinovka, Donetsk Oblast. Beskorovayni was allegedly subjected to enforced disappearance by the SBU, beaten and threatened during an interrogation, and held incommunicado for 15 months at an SBU facility in Kharkiv before being released on February 24 on the condition that he not speak about his detention. During his detention SBU officials repeatedly denied to Beskorovayni's family and human rights organizations that he was in SBU custody.

On August 28, HRW and AI released a statement in which they said that, since their initial report in July, 13 individuals had been released from the SBU facility in Kharkiv. The NGOs believed that at least five persons remained confined at the site. They noted that, once individuals had been released, local police simply closed their "missing persons" cases without further investigation.

Human rights groups reported that Russian-backed separatists routinely kidnapped persons for political purposes, to settle vendettas, or for ransom. HRW reported the arbitrary detentions of civilians by Russian-backed separatist forces, "which operate without any checks and balances." The HRMMU noted in its September report that these kidnappings were "spreading fear among civilians, in particular because of the arbitrary nature of abductions." The HRMMU also documented an increase in disappearances at checkpoints controlled by Russian-backed separatist forces. For example, on May 27, a former armed group member went missing in Novoluhanske, while travelling from government-controlled territory, where he had been detained by government forces. His mother later found that Russian-backed separatists had detained him at a checkpoint, transported him to Horlivka, and later transferred him to "police custody" in Donetsk. On July 4, "police" told her that they no longer held her son. She has since been unable to ascertain his fate or whereabouts.

On January 27, Russian-backed separatists abducted religious historian and president of the Center for Religious Studies and International Spiritual Relations, Ihor Kozlovsky, allegedly in retaliation for his pro-Ukrainian postings on social media. According to Kozlovsky's wife, the abductors confiscated keys to his apartment, which they then searched twice, removing equipment, documents, and a valuable collection of antique objects. According to local media, as of late November, Kozlovsky was being held in one of the separatists' informal detention centers in Donetsk.

Russian-backed separatists also abducted journalists attempting to cover the conflict. On March 3, they released abducted pro-Ukrainian journalist, Maria Varfolomeyeva, in a prisoner exchange after 14 months of captivity in Luhansk.

The politically motivated trial in Russia of Nadiya Savchenko, a military pilot and member of the Verkhovna Rada abducted from eastern Ukraine in 2014, ended in March with a guilty verdict and a 22-year prison sentence. On May 25, after almost two years of detention, Russian authorities exchanged Savchenko for two Russian soldiers (see section 1.e., Political Prisoners and Detainees, of the *Country Reports on Human Rights* for Russia).

<u>Physical Abuse, Punishment, and Torture</u>: Government and Russian-backed separatist forces reportedly abused and tortured civilians and soldiers in detention facilities. Reported abuses included beatings, physical and psychological torture, mock executions, sexual violence, deprivation of food and water, refusal of medical care, and forced labor.

The HRMMU received reports that government forces committed human rights violations, allegedly including forced deprivation of liberty and torture.

In its September report, the HRMMU noted that in the three-month reporting period reflected in the report, approximately 70 percent of cases documented by OHCHR contained allegations of torture, mistreatment, and incommunicado detention by SBU and other security forces prior to transfer into the criminal justice system. The September report did not provide data on the total number of such cases.

There were reports that Russian-backed separatist forces systematically committed numerous abuses, including torture, in the territories under their control. According to international organizations and NGOs, abuses included beatings, forced labor, psychological and physical torture, public humiliation, and sexual violence.

The HRMMU expressed repeated concern about reports of torture taking place in detention facilities controlled by Russian-backed separatists, to which they did not have access, and noted that reports of torture often surfaced long after the abuses had allegedly taken place. For example, the HRMMU's June report documented multiple new accounts of mock executions, severe beatings, and intentional deprivation of medical care from 2015. On September 23, in connection with the SPT's second visit to Ukraine, the SBU published a set of interviews with 11 individuals who alleged that they had been tortured while in the custody of Russian-backed separatists. The SBU also published a list of eight alleged torture sites in Donbas that it reported were controlled by Russian-backed separatists.

The HRMMU continued to document cases on both sides of the line of contact of sexual and gender-based violence of conflict-related detainees, both men and women. In its December report, the HRMMU noted: "In addition to a continuing pattern of sexual violence occurring in conflict-related detention, OHCHR documented cases that indicate the sexual violence and harassment of young women at government-controlled entry/exit checkpoints along the contact line."

According to the Justice for Peace in Donbas human rights coalition, individuals held in illegal detention facilities in territories controlled by Russian-backed separatists reported cases of gender-based violence, in particular rape, attempted rape, and sexual abuse.

The HRMMU was unable to obtain first-hand accounts of sexual violence in such areas but reported that it had received multiple secondary accounts. For example, a man detained by militants between March and April in an area of Donetsk controlled by Russian-backed separatists told the HRMMU about two women who were reportedly abducted at a checkpoint when coming from government-controlled territory and incarcerated in a room next to his. The detainee heard armed men harassing the women and attempting to rape them; two days later the women were relocated. Their identities or whereabouts were unknown to the interviewee.

Both sides employed land mines without measures to prevent civilian casualties. The HRMMU reported in June that "mines contaminate large areas of agricultural land in east Ukraine, often in areas which are poorly marked, near roads and surrounding civilian areas. This has resulted in civilians being killed and maimed, often while walking to their homes and fields. These risks are particularly acute for persons living in towns and settlements near the contact line, as well as the 23,000 people" who crossed the contact line every day between February and May.

According to the NGO Donbas SOS, approximately 27 square miles of territory in Donetsk and Luhansk Oblasts were in need of humanitarian demining. According to the Ministry of Defense, since the start of the conflict, 150 civilians have been killed and 500 injured by mines and other ordnance in the conflict zone.

<u>Child Soldiers</u>: There were no media reports of child soldiers serving with government forces, and the UN Children's Fund (UNICEF) could not confirm the presence of child soldiers in the country. There were media reports that government authorities had detained 17 persons between the ages of 15 and 18 who had fought with Russian-backed separatist forces since the beginning of the conflict in 2014. Russian-backed separatist news sources continued to cite the voluntary recruitment of children as young as 12 into the armed groups. In a January 22 interview in the newspaper *Dzerkalo Tizhdnya*, the head of the SBU's Antiterrorism Center, Vitaliy Malykov, described the Russian-backed separatist St. George the Victor battalion, in which he alleged that children between the ages of 12 and 16 were serving.

A three-month-long study by the Justice for Peace in Donbas coalition found that Russian aggression in Donbas has significantly increased the risk of children participating in armed conflict. The group's analysis of open sources and interviews revealed 41 individual cases of recruitment of children into armed formations. Of these, most were boys 16 to 17 years old participating in armed formations in territories of the Donetsk and Luhansk regions controlled by Russian-backed separatists.

<u>Other Conflict Related Abuses</u>: On September 28, a team of prosecutors from the Netherlands, Australia, Belgium, Malaysia, and Ukraine presented the results of their investigation of the 2014 downing of Malaysian Airlines Flight MH-17. The Dutch-led investigation concluded that the surface-to-air missile system used to shoot down the airliner over Ukraine, killing all 298 persons on board, was trucked in from Russia at the request of Russian-backed separatists and returned to Russia the same night. The report largely confirmed the already widely documented Russian government role in the deployment of the missile system, a Buk or SA-11, and the subsequent cover-up. In the report Dutch prosecutors traced Russia's role in deploying the missile system into Ukraine and its attempt to hide its role after the disaster.

In 2015 government authorities introduced measures to expedite the delivery of humanitarian aid to areas controlled by Russian-backed separatist forces. Russian-backed separatists in Donetsk Oblast, however, sharply restricted government humanitarian aid as well as aid from international humanitarian organizations. As a result persons remaining in territories held by Russian-backed separatists experienced large price increases for everyday consumables, especially meat and fresh vegetables. Human rights groups reported severe shortages of medicine and medical supplies in territory not controlled by the government.

Russian-backed separatists continued to receive convoys of Russian "humanitarian aid," which Ukrainian government officials believed contained weapons and supplies for combined Russian and separatist forces.

On February 11, HRW released a report, *Studying under Fire*, documenting "attacks on schools on both sides of the line of contact and the use of schools by both sides for military purposes, which has turned schools into legitimate military targets." The report also described 15 attacks on operating schools that were not being used as positions by the military.

Treatment for persons living with HIV and tuberculosis was disrupted in the east of the country where fighting interrupted crucial medical supplies. More than 6,000 persons living with HIV in the region struggled with a shortage of medicine and doctors.

Section 2. Respect for Civil Liberties, Including:

a. Freedom of Speech and Press

The constitution and law provide for freedom of speech and press, but authorities did not always respect these rights. The government introduced measures that banned or blocked information, media outlets, or individual journalists deemed a threat to national security or who expressed positions that authorities believed undermined the country's sovereignty and territorial integrity.

Other problematic practices continued to affect media freedom, including self-censorship, so-called jeansa payments to journalists for favorable news reports disguised as objective journalism, and slanted news coverage by media whose owners had close ties to the government or opposition political parties.

In the Donbas region, Russian-backed separatists suppressed freedom of speech and the press through harassment, intimidation, abductions, and assaults on journalists and media outlets. They also prevented the transmission of Ukrainian and independent television and radio programming in areas under their control.

<u>Freedom of Speech and Expression</u>: With some exceptions, individuals in areas not under Russian occupation or Russian-backed separatist control could generally criticize the government publicly and privately and discuss matters of public interest without fear of official reprisal. The law criminalizes the display of communist and Nazi symbols, although there have been no prosecutions.

The law prohibits statements that threaten the country's territorial integrity, promote war, instigate racial or religious conflict, or support Russian aggression towards Ukraine.

On September 15, the National Television and Radio Council issued a warning to Kherson-based radio station AKS for statements suggesting that Crimean Tatars were involved in terrorism. If a station receives a second warning, it could lose its broadcasting license.

On December 9, the Verkhovna Rada passed a bill to restrict imports of certain Russian books with "anti-Ukrainian content" that violated Ukrainian law. The books may still be legally imported below the commercial threshold of 100 copies.

<u>Press and Media Freedoms</u>: According to the NGO Freedom House, the press in the country was "partly free."

Independent media and internet news sites were active and expressed a wide range of views. Privately owned media, the most successful of which were generally owned by wealthy and influential "oligarchs," often presented readers and viewers a "biased pluralism," representing the views of their owners, favorable coverage of their allies, and criticizing political and business rivals. The 10 most popular television stations were owned by businessmen whose primary business was not in media. Independent media had difficulty competing with major outlets that operated with oligarchic subsidies.

The public television broadcaster was established in 2015 and planned to be fully operational by January 2017. On November 1, the head of the public broadcaster, Zurab Alasania, resigned from his position in protest regarding a number of obstacles to establishing the channel's operations, including the government's diversion of the channel's budget for other purposes. Alasania also cited complaints he had received from the government regarding investigative journalism programs on corruption produced by the broadcaster.

The practice of jeansa, or publishing unsubstantiated news articles for a fee, continued to be widespread. For example, according to the Institute of Mass Information press monitoring, the highest proportion of jeansa in regional media was found in print outlets in Mykolaiv Oblast, where 15 percent of all published articles were political or commercial jeansa.

Violence and Harassment: Violence against journalists remained a problem in the country, though attacks on journalists dropped for the second year. Human rights groups and journalists criticized government inaction in solving these crimes, giving rise to a culture of impunity.

According to the Institute of Mass Information, there were 30 reports of attacks on journalists, half as many as in 2015, and almost a 10th as many as in 2014. As in 2015, the majority of these attacks were perpetrated by private, not state, actors. There were 42 incidents of threats against and harassment of journalists, up from 36 in 2015.

The Institute of Mass Information and editors of major independent news outlets noted online harassment of journalists by societal actors, reflecting a growing societal intolerance of reporting deemed insufficiently patriotic, a development they said had the tacit support of the government. In one case, on May 10, the nationalist website *Myrotvorets* (Peacemaker), which allegedly has links to the Interior Ministry, published the names and personal information of more than 4,000 domestic and foreign journalists who had received accreditation from the Russian-backed separatist "authorities" in Donetsk and Luhansk. The website claimed that the journalists' actions amounted to collaboration with terrorists. On May 24, *Myrotvorets* published the personal information of an additional 300 journalists. Some affected media professionals subsequently received death threats and were subjected to significant online harassment. While Minister of Internal Affairs Arsen Avakov spoke out in support of *Myrotvorets*, calling the journalists "liberal separatists," President Poroshenko on June 3 condemned the website during his annual press conference. Police investigation of the case continued through year's end.

There were multiple incidents of violence and harassment against the television channel INTER, which is perceived to have a pro-Russian editorial policy.

According to press reports, in January protesters spray-painted "Kremlin mouthpiece" on INTER's offices and threw rocks through its windows. On February 25, volunteer Azov Battalion fighters blocked journalists' access to INTER's offices after INTER broadcasters were inadvertently recorded criticizing the "heavenly hundred," demonstrators killed during the Euromaidan protests. In June, protesters burned tires at the entrance to INTER's offices. On August 4, *Myrotvorets* published hacked email correspondence purporting to show that an INTER TV journalist had coordinated the contents of an article with Russian-backed separatist leaders. On August 31, Minister of Internal Affairs Arsen Avakov publicly called on the SBU to deal with INTER, which he labeled "anti-Ukrainian." On September 4, approximately 15 to 20 masked persons entered INTER's offices, setting fire to the building, destroying equipment, and trapping employees in the smoke-filled building. As a result some staff members were hospitalized, including one with a spinal injury. Authorities arrested six persons at the scene; an investigation into the attack by the SBU Investigative Department continued. On November 21, five unidentified persons threw Molotov cocktails at INTER's headquarters. Authorities opened an investigation into the incident, which continued at year's end.

On July 20, well-known journalist Pavel Sheremet, who hosted a morning show on Vesti radio and worked for the *Ukrainska Pravda* online news outlet, was killed by a bomb in the car he was driving in downtown Kyiv (see section 1.a.).

During the year authorities detained but later released two suspects in the 2015 killing in Kyiv of Oles Buzina, who was perceived as pro-Russian. Both suspects were allegedly members of right-wing political groups. An investigation into the case remained open at year's end.

There were multiple reports of attacks on journalists investigating government corruption. On May 24, three masked men fled in a car after beating Anatoliy Ostapenko, a journalist affiliated with the independent media outlet *Hromadske Zaporizhzhya*. Ostapenko was working on several investigations linking local authorities in Zaporizhzhya to corruption. An investigation into the attack continued at year's end.

<u>Censorship or Content Restrictions</u>: The Institute for Mass Information recorded seven incidents of censorship of individual publications, down from 12 in 2015.

Both independent and state-owned media periodically engaged in self-censorship when reporting stories that might expose political allies to criticism or that might be perceived by the public as insufficiently patriotic or that might provide information that could be used for Russian propaganda.

Libel/Slander Laws: Libel is a civil offense. While the law limits the monetary damages a plaintiff can claim in a lawsuit, local media observers continued to express concern over high monetary damages awarded for alleged libel. Government entities, and public figures in particular, used the threat of civil suits, sometimes based on alleged damage to a person's "honor and integrity," to influence or intimidate the press and investigative journalists. For example, on August 29, former prosecutor general, Viktor Shokin, announced he would sue the investigative journalism television program "Schemes" over its claims to have uncovered evidence of his corruption, including his ownership of luxury property registered in the names of family members.

National Security: Authorities took measures to prohibit, regulate, and occasionally censor information deemed a national security threat.

The government continued the practice of banning specific works by pro-Russian actors, film directors, and singers, as well as imposing sanctions on pro-Russian journalists. According to the head of the State Film Agency, Fillip Ilienko, as of February 18, some 432 films and television shows had been banned in the country on national security grounds since August 2014. On May 31, the president signed a decree imposing visa bans on 17 Russian journalists; several dozen other journalists were sanctioned previously. The decree also lifted sanctions against 29 foreign journalists. Human rights NGOs criticized the move. The Committee to Protect Journalists called on the country to "immediately rescind the decree banning Russian journalists from the country and to resist the urge to fight propaganda with censorship."

The government continued to block Russian television channels from broadcasting in the country, based on a 2014 decision by the National Television and Radio Broadcasting Council based on the perceived dangerous influence of Russian propaganda. As of year's end, only six Russian channels were permitted to broadcast, compared to 83 Russian channels able to broadcast in the country at the start of 2014. According to the head of the National Television and Radio Broadcasting Council, as of November 2, the council had issued 23 warnings to Ukrainian cable providers for violating the ban on certain Russian channels.

Media professionals continued to experience pressure from SBU and the armed forces when reporting on sensitive issues, such as military losses. On July 8, the press center of the Antiterrorist Operation (ATO) asked the SBU to suspend the accreditation of journalists representing two Ukrainian and one Russian media outlets that were reporting from Avdiivka, Donetsk Oblast. The journalists had released a video considered by the ATO headquarters to violate the rules for reporting from a conflict area, since it disclosed soldiers' faces, locations, and weaponry. After the request to remove it, the Ukrainian *Hromadske* journalists removed the video from their YouTube channel, but Russian journalist, Yulia Polukhina, published the material in *Novaya Gazeta*. After later receiving concurrence, *Hromadske* published an abridged version of the video approximately three weeks later. The HRMMU considered the response of the ATO headquarters to be disproportionate to the violation.

On February 24, the SBU deported Russian journalist, Mariya Stolyarova, and banned her from re-entering the country for five years. Stolyarova worked as a broadcast editor of "Podrobnosti Nedeli" ("Details of the Week") at INTER TV. Before the deportation the SBU conducted an investigation regarding an obscene statement Stolyarova made on air during a broadcast of material related to the "heavenly hundred" protesters who were killed during the Euromaidan demonstrations. Law enforcement officers also questioned Stolyarova's stay on territory controlled by Russian-backed separatists in eastern Ukraine and her alleged coordination of storylines with Russian-backed separatists.

Nongovernmental Impact: Russian-backed separatists in eastern areas of the country harassed, arbitrarily detained, and mistreated journalists (see section 1.g.). According to the HRMMU, "persons living in the 'Donetsk People's Republic' and 'Luhansk People's Republic' know that expressing their opinion freely and publicly was not acceptable in armed group-controlled territory," that "armed groups are directly influencing and shaping the content in local media," and that they require favorable coverage as the cost of retaining registration to operate.

According to the HRMMU and media reports, on January 4, the "Ministry of State Security" of the "Donetsk People's Republic" detained Kyiv-based blogger and activist, Volodymyr Fomichev, and charged him with unlawful possession of weapons. On June 27, he pled guilty and was sentenced to two years in prison. Fomichev's family insisted the conviction was baseless and the result of a forced confession. During the "hearings," Fomichev gave his father a sweater covered with blood, raising concerns about mistreatment by "investigators."

Actions to Expand Press Freedom: On February 4, parliament passed a law criminalizing the illegal seizure of materials collected, processed, and prepared by journalists or of technical devices they use in their professional activities. The law also introduces a penalty of up to three years' imprisonment for unlawfully denying journalists access to information, unlawfully banning them from covering particular topics, or for any other action impeding their professional activity.

Internet Freedom

Authorities did not restrict or disrupt access to the internet or censor online content. Law enforcement bodies monitored the internet, at times without appropriate legal authority. Authorities did not restrict content or censor websites or other communications and internet services.

According to the International Telecommunication Union, 49 percent of persons in the country used the internet in 2015.

Human rights groups and journalists that were critical of Russian involvement in the Donbas region and Crimea reported that opponents subjected their websites to cyberattacks, such as coordinated denial of service incidents and unauthorized attempts to obtain information from computers, as well as coordinated campaigns of "trolling" and harassment on social media.

Users of social media, particularly Facebook and *VKontakte*, sometimes had their access temporarily blocked for innocuous or political posts that other users mischaracterized as "hate speech" and flagged as terms of service violations.

In its yearly *Freedom on the Net* report, Freedom House assessed in November that internet freedom in the country deteriorated for the second year in a row, noting that, "Ukrainian authorities have become less tolerant of online expression perceived as critical of Ukraine's position in the conflict, and the government has been especially active this year in sanctioning social media users for 'separatist' and "extremist" activities, with many users detained, fined and even imprisoned for such activities. Meanwhile, Russian-backed separatist forces in the east have stepped up efforts to block content online perceived to be in support of Ukrainian government or cultural identity."

Academic Freedom and Cultural Events

There were several reports of government restrictions on academic freedom or cultural events. On November 4, the SBU announced that it had banned 140

Russian cultural figures from entering the country, as their actions or statements conflicted with the country's interests.

b. Freedom of Peaceful Assembly and Association

Freedom of Assembly

The constitution provides citizens with the right to freedom of assembly, and the government generally respected this right. There are no laws, however, regulating the process of organizing and conducting events to provide for freedom of peaceful assembly. Authorities have wide discretion under a Soviet-era directive to grant or refuse permission for assemblies on grounds of protecting public order and safety. Organizers are required to inform authorities in advance of plans for protests or demonstrations.

During the year citizens generally exercised the right to peaceful assembly without restriction in areas of the country under government control. Most assemblies were peaceful and at times accompanied by a very large police presence to maintain order. The HRMMU noted an overall improvement in the ability of the National Police to provide security for demonstrations.

There were some reports of violence at LGBTI demonstrations during the year (see section 6.).

On July 4, more than 100 persons protested peacefully against the presence of military equipment in Toretsk, Donetsk Oblast. Police arrested eight men, charged them with disobeying police, interrogated them without lawyers present, and did not bring them before the court within three hours, as required by the law. SBU officers reportedly threatened and intimidated the detainees. The detainees spent the night sleeping on the floor of a small cell with only one mattress and a wooden bench. After the court hearing ordering their release, they were brought back to a police station where the head of police in the Donetsk Oblast allegedly insulted and threatened them before their release.

In the territory controlled by Russian-backed separatists, the HRMMU noted an absence of demonstrations because "people are concerned that they may be 'arrested' if they organize protests or assemblies against the policies of the armed groups." The HRMMU also noted that the only demonstrations permitted in these areas were ones in support of local authorities, often apparently organized by the armed groups, with forced public participation.

Freedom of Association

The constitution and law provide for freedom of association, and the government generally respected this right.

The HRMMU noted a pattern of harassment of Communist Party members. For example, on June 28, the apartment of a first secretary of the Kharkiv local branch of the Communist Party was searched, and she was charged with violating the territorial integrity of Ukraine and bribing state officials. On June 30, a Kharkiv court ruled to place her in pretrial detention.

According to the HRMMU, in the territories controlled by the Russian-backed separatists, "civil society organizations, including human rights defenders, cannot operate freely." Residents informed the HRMMU that they were being prosecuted (or were afraid of being prosecuted) by the "ministry of state security" for their pro-Ukrainian views or previous affiliation with Ukrainian NGOs. The HRMMU also noted an increase in civil society organizations run by the armed groups, which appeared to have compulsory membership for certain persons, such as public sector employees.

c. Freedom of Religion

See the Department of State's *International Religious Freedom Report* at www.state.gov/religiousfreedomreport/.

d. Freedom of Movement, Internally Displaced Persons, Protection of Refugees, and Stateless Persons

The constitution and law provide citizens with freedom of internal movement, foreign travel, emigration, and repatriation. The government, however, restricted these rights, particularly in the eastern part of the country near the zone of conflict.

Abuse of Migrants, Refugees, and Stateless Persons: Authorities frequently detained asylum seekers for extended periods without court approval.

The government cooperated with the Office of UNHCR and other humanitarian organizations in providing protection and assistance to internally displaced persons (IDPs), refugees, returning refugees, asylum seekers, stateless persons, and other persons of concern. International and domestic organizations reported the system for protecting asylum seekers, stateless persons, and other persons of concern did not operate effectively.

<u>In-country Movement</u>: The government and Russian-backed separatist forces strictly controlled the freedom of movement between government- and Russian-backed separatist controlled territories in the Donbas region. Crossing the contact line remained arduous. While five crossing points existed, only four were in operation for much of the year. According to the HRMMU, between May and August, an average of 26,000 to 32,000 individuals crossed the line daily. People formed long lines at all operating transit corridors and had to wait for up to 36 hours with no or limited access to water, medical aid, toilets, and shelter in case of shelling or extreme weather. The HRMMU's March report noted that two elderly persons died at government checkpoints due to lack of timely medical care; its September report noted three deaths for the same reason. The HRMMU's June report noted that, on April 27, four civilians were killed and eight injured at a crossing point near Olenivka in the "Donetsk People's Republic," when it was shelled while they waited in line overnight.

Movement across the line of contact was limited to four crossing points in Donetsk Oblast and one in Luhansk Oblast, which were frequently closed due to nearby fighting. The crossing point at Stanytsia Luhanska traversed a temporary wooden structure that the OSCE Special Monitoring Mission (SMM) believed was unsafe. People regularly reported long lines; as an example, on August 19, the SMM reported more than 700 persons waiting to cross into the country at Stanytsia Luhanska. On August 16, more than 1,000 persons were observed at the same crossing point, and medical officials claimed 21 persons were treated for heat-related illnesses.

In 2015 the SBU introduced a pass system involving an online application process to control movement into government-controlled territory. Human rights groups were concerned that many persons in nongovernment-controlled territory did not have access to the internet to obtain such passes. The order imposed significant hardships on persons crossing into government-controlled territory, in particular those who sought to receive pensions and government benefits, which ceased distribution in the territory controlled by Russian-backed separatists in 2014.

The HRMMU repeatedly voiced concern about reports of corruption by checkpoint personnel on both sides, including demands for bribes or goods in exchange for easing passage across the line of contact. Russian-backed separatists continued to hinder freedom of movement in the eastern part of the country during the year. In

April the crossing checkpoint in Stanytsia Luhanska was closed due to shelling by Russian-backed separatist forces and, as of December, it was open only for pedestrians. Russian-backed separatists have also consistently prevented civilians from crossing at the Zolote checkpoint in Luhansk oblast.

The government and Russian occupation authorities subjected individuals crossing between Russian-occupied Crimea and the mainland to strict passport controls at the administrative boundary between the Kherson oblast and Crimea. Authorities prohibited rail and commercial bus service across the administrative boundary, requiring persons either to cross on foot or by private vehicle. The three crossing points between Russian-occupied Crimea and mainland Ukraine were closed on several occasions in early August, creating long lines of individuals who were prevented from freely moving across the administrative boundary. As of August 15, the movement of vehicles and persons fully resumed but slowed due to enhanced security measures.

Internally Displaced Persons

According to the Ministry of Social Policy, as of November 15, there were more than 1.7 million registered internally displaced persons (IDPs) due to Russia's aggression in eastern Ukraine and occupation of Crimea. Some NGOs and international organizations estimated the number to be lower, since some persons returned to their homes after registering as IDPs, while others registered while still living in the conflict zone. The largest number of IDPs resided in areas immediately surrounding the conflict zones, in government-controlled areas of Donetsk and Luhansk Oblasts, as well as in the Kharkiv, Dnipropetrovsk, and Zaporizhzhya Oblasts. Many resided in areas close to the line of contact in hope that they would be able to return home.

The government granted social entitlements only to those individuals who had registered as IDPs. By law IDPs are eligible to receive payments of 880 hryvnias ($33) per month for children and persons with disabilities and 440 hryvnias ($16) per month for those able to work. Families may receive no more than 2,400 hryvnias ($89) per month. According to the law, the government should provide IDPs with housing, but authorities had not taken effective steps to do so. Humanitarian aid groups had good access to areas under government control.

On February 16, the Ministry of Social Policy instructed its regional offices and local departments to suspend all social payments for IDPs, pending verification of their presence in government-controlled territory, ostensibly to combat fraudulent payments. According to the HRMMU, following this decision the SBU provided regional administrations with lists of individuals whose social entitlements should be revoked pending verification. The HRMMU reviewed a list that the SBU submitted to the regional administration in Kharkiv and determined that it was developed from information in the SBU database on individuals who received permits to cross the contact line. On June 8, the government adopted amendments to resolutions on IDPs to allow for automatic termination of benefits and prescribing two to six months for reinstatement, depending on the grounds for termination. The HRMMU, the human rights ombudsperson, the Council of Europe, and other domestic and international human rights and humanitarian groups criticized these amendments.

According to the HRMMU, the government applied the IDP verification procedure extremely broadly. The suspensions affected approximately 85 percent of IDPs residing in government-controlled areas and 97 percent of those residing in areas under the control of Russian-backed separatists, particularly the elderly and disabled whose limited mobility hindered their ability to verify whether they were included in the lists or prove their residency. The government often suspended payments without notification, and IDPs reported problems having them reinstated. In one case the HRMMU interviewed a female IDP with disabilities in Kramatorsk, who was also the single parent of a 13-year-old daughter with disabilities. She incidentally discovered that all of her other social payments had also been cut, including her disability pension.

According to the HRMMU, IDP integration remained impeded by the lack of a state strategy and the consequent absence of allocation of financial resources, leading to IDPs' economic and social marginalization. Local civil society organizations and international humanitarian organizations provided the bulk of assistance for IDPs on a temporary basis. NGOs reported that their ability to support IDPs was limited and nearing exhaustion. UN agencies reported that the influx of IDPs led to tensions arising from competition for resources. Critics accused internally displaced men who moved to western areas of the country of evading military service, while competition rose for housing, employment, and educational opportunities in Kyiv and Lviv.

A shortage of employment opportunities and the generally weak economy particularly affected IDPs, forcing many to live in inadequate housing, such as collective centers and other temporary accommodation. As of July 1, there were 271 such collective centers housing more than 10,000 persons. Other IDPs stayed with host families, volunteers, and in private accommodation, although affordable private accommodation was often in poor condition.

UN agencies expressed concern about instances of eviction of IDPs from the collective centers. On September 29, 22 elderly IDPs, including two disabled persons, were evicted from the Kuialnyk sanatorium in Odesa. A representative from the Odesa regional administration stated that the management of the sanatorium had suspended utilities on September 26 due to nonpayment of bills. While collective center accommodation was only intended as a temporary solution, many IDPs remained for extended periods.

There were reports of government officials expressing discriminatory views toward IDPs. For example, on September 23, Minister of Internal Affairs Avakov publicly attributed an increase in the crime rate to an inflow of IDPs, provoking a public outcry.

NGOs reported employment discrimination against IDPs. Some IDPs, particularly those in government-controlled areas of Donetsk and Luhansk Oblasts, lacked sufficient sanitation, shelter, and access to potable water. IDPs continued to have difficulty obtaining education, medical care, and necessary documents. Romani activists expressed concern that some Roma in eastern areas could not afford to flee conflict areas, while others had no choice but to leave their homes.

In September 2015 the Kyiv Administrative Court of Appeal overturned a National Bank decision that Crimean IDPs were nonresidents, which had restricted access to banking and financial services for those fleeing the Russian occupation. Nonetheless, media reports indicated that banks continued to restrict banking services for Crimean IDPs even after the court decision.

Protection of Refugees

<u>Access to Asylum</u>: The law provides for asylum or refugee status, and the government has established a legal system to protect refugees. Protection for refugees and asylum seekers was insufficient due to gaps in the law and the system of implementation. The country is a transit and destination country for asylum seekers and refugees, principally from Afghanistan, Somalia, and Syria.

Human rights groups noted that the refugee law falls short of international standards due to its restrictive definition of who is a refugee. The law permits authorities to reject many asylum applications without a thorough case assessment.

In other instances government officials declined to accept initial asylum applications without a legal basis, leaving asylum seekers without documentation and vulnerable to frequent police stops, fines, detention, and exploitation. Asylum seekers in detention centers were sometimes unable to apply for refugee status within the prescribed time limits and had limited access to legal and other assistance. Asylum seekers have five days to appeal an order of detention or deportation.

A lack of access to qualified interpreters also hampered the full range of asylum procedures. International observers noted that the government did not provide resources for interpreters, which created opportunities for corruption and undermined the fairness of asylum application procedures.

Refoulement: The government did not provide for protection against the expulsion or return of asylum seekers to a country where there was reason to believe their lives or freedom would be threatened on account of their race, religion, nationality, membership in a particular social group, or political opinion. UNHCR described refoulement at the border as a "largely hidden phenomenon," as persons seeking asylum may not receive legal aid or interpretation at border crossing points or temporary holding facilities and were, therefore, unable to apply for asylum before being deported. Human rights groups noted the law offers legal protection against forcible return.

Employment: Authorities did not provide employment assistance, and most asylum seekers were unable to obtain a work permit as required by law. Authorities provided language instruction for asylum seekers only in Kyiv, Kharkiv, and Odesa. Some attempted to work illegally, increasing their risk of exploitation.

Access to Basic Services: The national plan on the integration of refugees adopted by the government did not allocate resources for its implementation. Human rights groups reported that authorities did not provide social and economic support to asylum seekers or assist them. Authorities did not provide language courses or social assistance. A UNHCR report indicated all newly recognized refugees received a one-time grant of approximately 30 hryvnias ($1.10).

Temporary accommodation centers had a reception capacity of 320 persons and could accommodate approximately 20 percent of asylum applicants. Asylum seekers living outside a center often experienced difficulties obtaining residence registration, and authorities regularly fined them more than 500 hryvnias ($19) because they lacked this registration. According to the State Migration Service, refugees and those seeking complementary protection could receive residence registration at homeless shelters for up to six months.

UNHCR noted an improvement in the quantity and quality of food provided in the migrant custody centers as well as a lack of educational programs and vocational activities for those in detention for extended periods. According to UNHCR, gaps in housing and social support for unaccompanied children left many without access to state-run accommodation centers or children's shelters. As of November 1, seven unaccompanied migrant children were registered, five of whom expressed a desire to apply for refugee status. Many children had to rely on informal networks for food, shelter, and other needs and remained vulnerable to abuse, trafficking, and other forms of exploitation.

Temporary Protection: The government also provided temporary protection ("complementary protection") to individuals who may not qualify as refugees; authorities provided it to approximately 618 persons during the year.

Stateless Persons

According to law, a person may acquire citizenship by birth, territorial origin, naturalization, restored citizenship, and adoption.

According to UNHCR, there were 35,179 persons in the country under its statelessness mandate as of mid-2015. According to the State Migration Service, at the end of the year there were 5,343 stateless persons residing in the country.

The law requires establishing identity through a court procedure, which demanded more time and money than some applicants had. UNHCR reported Roma were at particular risk for statelessness, since many did not have birth certificates or any other types of documentation to verify their identity.

Section 3. Freedom to Participate in the Political Process

The constitution and law provide citizens the ability to choose their government in free and fair periodic elections held by secret ballot and based on universal and equal suffrage. On July 17, parliamentary by-elections were conducted in seven constituencies.

Elections and Political Participation

<u>Recent Elections</u>: In 2014 citizens elected Petro Poroshenko president in an election considered free and fair by international and domestic observers. Later that year the country held early parliamentary elections that observers also considered free and fair. In October 2015 the country held nationwide local elections.

On July 17, citizens in seven constituencies voted in parliamentary by-elections. According to the OSCE observer mission, the elections were organized and democratic but influenced by economic interests. According to OPORA, a human rights NGO that monitored elections in the country, some candidates started campaigning prematurely, leading to unfair advantages for certain candidates and parties. OPORA considered the elections to be free and fair with electoral irregularities that were not systemic.

IDPs were unable to vote in local elections unless they changed their registration to their new place of residence.

<u>Political Parties and Political Participation</u>: On February 25, President Poroshenko signed a bill that allows political parties to wait until after an election to select which members from a party list will take seats in the Verkhovna Rada. The law was widely criticized by domestic and international election monitoring groups, as it shifts the power of selecting deputies from the electorate to the leadership of political parties.

The Communist Party remains banned.

<u>Participation of Women and Minorities</u>: There are no laws limiting the participation of women and members of minorities in the political process and women and minorities did so.

Section 4. Corruption and Lack of Transparency in Government

The law provides criminal penalties for corruption, although authorities did not effectively implement the law, and many officials engaged in corrupt practices with impunity. While the number of reports of government corruption was low, corruption remained pervasive at all levels in the executive, legislative, and judicial branches of government and in society.

During the year multiple high-level officials who had been brought into the government to oversee anticorruption reform processes resigned due to efforts to impede their work. Complaining of ingrained corruption, Minister of Economy Aivaras Abromavicius resigned in February and was followed by some members of his team. Abromavicius stated in his resignation letter that corrupt officials had blocked systematic reform and were attempting to gain influence over state enterprises.

Corruption: While the government publicized several attempts to combat corruption, it remained a serious problem for citizens and businesses alike. The law establishes two governmental anticorruption bodies, the National Agency for Prevention of Corruption (NAPC) and the National Anticorruption Bureau of Ukraine (NABU).

As of October 1, the NABU had launched 243 criminal proceedings in corruption cases with support from the newly created Specialized Anticorruption Prosecutor's Office. Authorities tried 31 corruption cases involving 70 persons, including judges, prosecutors, and state officers, but many were for minor violations. In a major anticorruption case, the Verkhovna Rada stripped Member of Parliament Oleksandr Onyshchenko of immunity from prosecution in July under suspicion of corruption and embezzlement. At year's end he remained a fugitive outside the country, and the investigation continued.

Civil society criticized the Prosecutor General's Office and the judicial system for failing to hold high-level officials to account for corruption. According to the anticorruption watchdog group, Nashi Hroshi, between July 2015 and July 2016, 952 persons were convicted of corruption. Of these individuals 312 were fined (70 percent of these fines were below 20,000 hryvnias ($740)), 336 persons received suspended sentences, and 137 had their convictions overturned. One hundred twenty-eight persons were sentenced to prison; of these individuals 33 were serving sentences, while the rest had appeals pending. Of the 952 persons convicted for corruption, only three were officials of significant stature: two heads of district administrations and one deputy head of the state agricultural inspectorate. As of July all three cases were undergoing appeals, and the defendants had yet to begin serving their sentences.

While members of the Verkhovna Rada are immune from prosecution, several members, such as Onyshchenko, were stripped of immunity for prosecution during the year. Judges may not be arrested or detained before courts convict them, unless the Verkhovna Rada rescinds their immunity.

The NAPC is responsible for the development of national anticorruption policies, monitoring national compliance with anticorruption legislation, and verifying asset declarations of high officials. The NAPC, established in March 2015, began operations in May.

The law designates NABU as the lead investigative agency for allegations of corruption by senior government officials, including the president, members of the Cabinet of Ministers, members of the Verkhovna Rada, and local governors. NABU is responsible only for investigating corruption offenses committed after its creation in 2015. The Prosecutor General's Office had 25,000 open corruption cases that predated the creation of NABU.

There were reports that the Prosecutor General's Office took steps during the year to hinder NABU's ability to investigate high-level corruption. On August 5, an investigative group from the Prosecutor General's Office raided the NABU headquarters in Kyiv, alleging that NABU had illegally wiretapped its employees. On August 12, Prosecutor General's Office staff allegedly unlawfully detained and beat two NABU detectives who they asserted were engaged in wiretapping. On September 20, three Prosecutor General's Office employees were suspended pending the outcome of an internal investigation, which continued at year's end.

According to the Justice Ministry, implementation of a 2014 law on "lustration" was 99 percent completed. Some 700,000 civil servants and state officials were on the list for lustration. The checks resulted in the dismissal of approximately 1,000 state officials. According to the Parliamentary Anticorruption Committee, 80 percent of state officials from the Yanukovych era were discharged from their posts. Law enforcement and judicial agencies, however, avoided full compliance with the law. The SBU subjected only 50 staff members to lustration. The judiciary lustrated only 40 judges, eight of whom contested the decision in court and were restored to their positions.

Financial Disclosure: The law mandates the filing of income and expenditure declarations by public officials, and a special review process allows for public access to declarations and sets penalties for either not filing or filing a false declaration.

By law, the NACP is responsible for reviewing financial declarations and monitoring the income and expenditures of high-level officials. On August 15, the government officially launched an asset e-declaration system. By the conclusion of the first phase on November 1, more than 120,000 officials had submitted e-declarations, indicating near total compliance. The results were made publicly available, provoking public outcry about the lavish lifestyles of many public officials. By law the NAPC reviews the declarations and refers suspected corruption cases to the NABU for further action. Some observers questioned, however, whether the NAPC had the capacity to fulfill this function.

<u>Public Access to Information</u>: The constitution and law require authorities to provide government information upon request, unless it pertains to national security. By law officials must respond to regular requests within five days and within 20 days to requests for large amounts of data. Requesters can appeal denials within agencies and ultimately to the court system. Instructions for filing information requests were a common and conspicuous component of government websites. Implementation of the law on public access to government information and training of officials on the regulations governing such access remained inadequate.

Section 5. Governmental Attitude Regarding International and Nongovernmental Investigation of Alleged Violations of Human Rights

A variety of domestic and international human rights groups generally operated without government restriction, investigating and publishing their findings on human rights cases. Government officials were cooperative and responsive to their views. The government invited human rights groups to participate in monitoring activities, drafting legislation, and adopting administrative rules.

International and domestic human rights groups collaborated with the government to draft the *National Human Rights Strategy* and related action plan in 2015. During the year civil society closely monitored implementation and expressed concern about government progress on the action plan. Representatives from the human rights ombudsman's office noted that, as of September 23, the strategy remained largely unimplemented and cited concerted resistance from certain ministries, including the Ministries of Justice and Health, to cooperating with the office on implementation. Human rights groups described particular government resistance to implementing points in the plan that related to the rights of IDPs. The HRMMU stated that, in the Ministry of Justice's first progress report on the plan, some activities marked as completed were implemented only partially or not in substance.

The Ministry of Justice, the Office of the Human Rights Ombudsman's, and civil society groups such as the Ukrainian Helsinki Human Rights Union participated in open hearings in December to mark the one-year anniversary of the action plan. Nongovernmental representatives reported slow progress and weak intragovernmental coordination, but both government representatives and human rights activists indicated progress in justice sector reform and the provision of social services.

Russian authorities and the separatists they backed routinely denied domestic and international human rights groups access to territories they controlled in Crimea and eastern Ukraine. If human rights groups attempted to work in those areas, they faced significant harassment and intimidation (see section 2.b.).

<u>The United Nations or Other International Bodies</u>: The government cooperated with international organizations, such as the OSCE, the Council of Europe, and the HRMMU.

<u>Government Human Rights Bodies</u>: The constitution provides for a human rights ombudsman, officially designated as parliamentary commissioner on human rights. The Human Rights Ombudsman's Office frequently collaborated with NGOs through civic advisory councils on various projects for monitoring human rights practices in prisons and other government institutions (see sections 1.c. and 1.d.).

Valeriya Lutkovska served as parliamentary ombudsman for human rights during the year, and observers considered her office an effective promoter of human rights. The office was a partner with leading domestic human rights groups and an advocate on behalf of Crimean Tatars, IDPs, Roma, persons with disabilities, LGBTI individuals, and prisoners.

Section 6. Discrimination, Societal Abuses, and Trafficking in Persons

Women

<u>Rape and Domestic Violence</u>: The law prohibits rape but does not explicitly address spousal rape. The courts may use a law against "forced sex with a materially dependent person" as grounds to prosecute spousal rape. Under the law authorities can detain a person for up to five days for offenses related to domestic violence and spousal abuse.

Sexual assault and rape continued to be significant but underreported problems. According to the Prosecutor General's Office, through September there were 355 registered reports of rape or attempted rape of which authorities brought 47 to court.

Domestic violence against women remained a serious problem. Spousal abuse was common. According to the Prosecutor General's Office, 922 cases of domestic violence were registered during the first nine months of the year, and 833 cases were brought to court. Advocacy groups asserted the percentage of women subjected to physical violence or psychological abuse at home remained high. Human rights groups noted the ability of agencies to detect and report cases of domestic violence was limited, and preventive services remained underfunded and underdeveloped. Additionally, human rights groups stated that law enforcement authorities did not consider domestic violence to be a serious crime but rather a private matter to be settled between spouses.

According to the Kyiv-based international women's rights center, La Strada, Russian aggression in the Donbas region led to a dramatic surge in violence against women across the country. Human rights groups attributed the increase in violence to post-traumatic stress experienced by IDPs fleeing the conflict and by soldiers returning from combat. IDPs reported instances of rape and sexual abuse; many claimed to have fled because they feared sexual abuse. There were no special social services available to women IDPs. According to the Ministry for Social Policy, police issued approximately 38,000 domestic violence warnings and protection orders during a six-month period. According to the ministry, approximately 65,000 persons were under police monitoring in connection with domestic violence. Punishment included fines, administrative arrest, and community service.

La Strada operated a national hotline for victims of violence and sexual harassment. Through September more than 24,000 individuals called the hotline for assistance, and 35 percent of the calls related to domestic or sexual violence. According to La Strada, more than 49 percent of calls related to psychological violence. The NGO reported that expanded public awareness campaigns increased the number of requests for assistance it received each year.

Although the law requires the government to operate a shelter in every major city, it did not do so, in part due to lack of municipal funding. During the year officials identified 19 centers for social and psychological help and nine centers for psychological and legal help for women who suffered from domestic violence.

According to the Ministry of Social Policy, as of July 1, government centers provided domestic violence-related services, in the form of sociopsychological assistance, to 423 families with children and 3,934 individuals. Social services centers monitored families in matters related to domestic violence and child abuse. NGOs operated additional centers for victims of domestic violence in several regions, but women's rights groups noted that many nongovernment shelters closed due to lack of funding.

According to women's advocacy groups, municipal and privately funded shelters were not always accessible. Shelters were frequently full, and resources were limited. Some shelters did not function throughout the year, and administrative restrictions prevented women and families from accessing services. For example, some shelters would only accept children of certain ages, while others did not admit women not registered as local residents. Government centers offered only limited legal, psychological, and economic assistance to survivors of domestic violence. Each center could accommodate approximately 30 women and children, which was often inadequate.

<u>Sexual Harassment</u>: The law puts sexual harassment in the same category as discrimination, but women's rights groups asserted there was no effective mechanism to protect against sexual harassment. They reported continuing and widespread sexual harassment, including coerced sex, in the workplace. Women rarely sought legal recourse because courts declined to hear their cases and rarely convicted perpetrators. Women's groups also cited a persistent culture of sexism and harassment.

While the law prohibits coercing a "materially dependent person" to have sexual intercourse, legal experts stated that safeguards against harassment were inadequate.

<u>Reproductive Rights</u>: The government recognized the right of couples and individuals to decide the number, spacing, and timing of their children, manage their reproductive health, and have the information and means to do so, free from discrimination, coercion, and violence.

<u>Discrimination</u>: The law provides that women enjoy the same rights as men, including under family, religious, personal status, labor, property, nationality, and inheritance laws, and are entitled to receive equal pay for equal work. In practice women received lower salaries than men (see section 7.d.).

Children

<u>Birth Registration</u>: Either birthplace or parentage determines citizenship. A child born to stateless parents residing permanently in the country is a citizen. The law requires that parents register a child within a month of birth.

Registration of children born in Crimea or areas in the east controlled by Russian-backed separatists remained difficult. Authorities required hospital paperwork to register births. Russian-backed separatist "authorities" routinely kept such paperwork if parents registered children in territories under their control, making it difficult for the child to obtain a Ukrainian birth certificate. Additionally, authorities do not recognize documents issued by Russian-occupied Crimean or Russian-backed separatist entities and sometimes refused to issue birth certificates to children born in those areas.

<u>Child Abuse</u>: As of September 30, the Ministry of Internal Affairs reported 4,817 crimes against children. Human rights groups noted that authorities lacked the capability to detect violence against children and refer victims for assistance. Preventive services remained underfunded and underdeveloped. There were also instances of forced labor involving children (see section 7.c.).

Authorities did not take effective measures at the national level to protect children from abuse and violence and to prevent such problems. Parliament's ombudsman for human rights noted the imperfection of mechanisms to protect children who survived violence or witnessed violence, in particular violence committed by their parents. According to the law parents were legal representatives of children, even if they perpetrated violence against them. There is no procedure for appointing a temporary legal representative of a child during the investigation of a case of parental violence.

The Office of the Parliamentary Ombudsman for Human Rights includes a representative for children's rights, nondiscrimination, and gender equality. As of August 31, the office had received 552 complaints regarding children's rights.

A major consequence of Russian aggression in the Donbas was its effect on children. In January the law On Protection of Childhood was amended to include a provision supporting children affected by the armed conflict. In August the Ukrainian Institute of Extremism Research reported that fighting killed 166 children since the conflict started in 2014. According to UNICEF the conflict has affected 1.7 million children, including approximately 230,000 forced from their homes. Children living in areas controlled by Russian-backed separatists did not receive nutritional and shelter assistance. Human rights groups reported that children who experienced the conflict or fled from territory controlled by Russian-backed separatists suffered psychological trauma. UNICEF reported that 200,000 children in the Donbas needed psychological rehabilitation, and approximately 580,000 urgently needed aid.

Early and Forced Marriage: The minimum age for marriage is 18. If it finds marriage to be in the child's interest, a court may grant a child as young as 16 permission to marry. Romani rights groups reported early marriages involving girls under the age of 18 were common in the Romani community.

Sexual Exploitation of Children: The law prohibits the commercial sexual exploitation of children, the sale of children, offering or procuring a child for child prostitution, and practices related to child pornography. The minimum prison sentence for child rape is 10 years. Molesting children under the age of 16 is punishable by imprisonment for up to five years. The same offense committed against a child under the age of 14 is punishable by imprisonment for five to eight years. The age of consent is 16.

The Ministry of Internal Affairs recorded 274 sexual crimes against children during the year. Sexual exploitation of children, however, remained significantly underreported. Commercial sexual exploitation of children remained a serious problem.

Domestic and foreign law enforcement officials reported that a significant amount of child pornography on the internet continued to originate in the country. The International Organization for Migration reported that children from socially disadvantaged families and those in state custody continued to be at high risk of trafficking and commercial sexual exploitation and the production of pornography. Courts may limit access to websites that disseminate child pornography and impose financial penalties and prison sentences on those operating the websites.

Child Soldiers: There were reports that Russian-backed separatists used child soldiers in the conflict in the east of the country (see section 1.g.).

Displaced Children: According to the Ministry of Social Policy, authorities registered more than 235,700 children as IDPs. Human rights groups believed this number was low, as children who fled without their parents cannot register as IDPs unless another relative officially files for custody, which can be a lengthy process. The majority of IDP children were from Donetsk and Luhansk Oblasts.

<u>Institutionalized Children</u>: The child welfare system continued to rely on long-term residential care for children at social risk or without parental care, although the number of residential care institutions continued to drop. During the year some 100,000 orphans and other children deprived of parental care lived and studied in various types of boarding schools. Approximately 90 percent of such children ended in the schools because of their parents' poverty, their inability to raise children, or the child's developmental disorders.

In recent years the government implemented policies to address the abandonment of children and their reintegration with their biological families. Consequently, the number of children deprived of parental care decreased. Human rights groups and media reported unsafe, inhuman, and sometimes life-threatening conditions in some institutions. Children institutionalized in state-run orphanages were at times vulnerable to trafficking. Officials of several state-run institutions and orphanages were allegedly complicit or willfully negligent in the sex and labor trafficking of girls and boys under their care.

Observers noted the judicial system lacked the expertise to work effectively with minors, and the legal process for juveniles emphasized punishment over rehabilitation. Supportive social services were often lacking, and children in custody or under supervision faced bureaucratic and social barriers to reintegration. Authorities viewed imprisonment as a form of supervision and punishment rather than correction and education.

<u>International Child Abductions</u>: The country is a party to the 1980 Hague Convention on the Civil Aspects of International Child Abduction. See the Department of State's *Annual Report on International Parental Child Abduction* at travel.state.gov/content/childabduction/en/legal/compliance.html.

Anti-Semitism

According to census data and international Jewish groups, an estimated 103,600 Jews lived in the country, constituting approximately 0.2 percent of the population. According to the Association of Jewish Organizations and Communities (VAAD), there were approximately 300,000 persons of Jewish ancestry in the country, although the number may be higher. Before Russian aggression in eastern Ukraine, according to VAAD approximately 30,000 Jewish persons lived in the

Donbas. Jewish groups estimated between 10,000 and 15,000 Jewish residents lived in Crimea before Russia's attempted annexation.

Jewish community leaders reported that societal anti-Semitism was low, and authorities took steps to address problems of anti-Semitism when they arose. Institutional anti-Semitism was rare, and VAAD stated that attacks were isolated and carried out by individuals rather than organized groups. VAAD claimed that negative attitudes towards Jews and Judaism continued to be low, although some individuals espoused anti-Semitic beliefs. VAAD believed that some attacks were provocations meant to discredit the government. In September the Jewish pilgrimage to the Uman burial site of Rabbi Nachman took place without significant incidents. On December 21, however, unknown individuals vandalized the site with a pig's head and blood. Authorities opened an investigation into the incident and immediately condemned it.

In July authorities named a street in Kyiv after former Organization of Ukrainian Nationalists (OUN) leader, Stepan Bandera. In response according to press reports, more than 20 Ukrainian Jewish groups published a statement condemning, as a form of Holocaust denial, the naming of streets for leaders of the OUN and the Ukrainian Insurgent Army (UPA),. Some international scholars also objected. At the same time, authorities also named a street in Kyiv in honor of Janusz Korczak, a Polish-Jewish writer who had died in Auschwitz.

According to the National Minority Rights Monitoring Group (NMRMG) supported by the Euro-Asian Jewish Congress and VAAD, one case of suspected anti-Semitic violence was recorded during the year, compared to one case of anti-Semitic violence in 2015, four such cases in 2014, and four in 2013. The NMRMG identified 18 cases of anti-Semitic vandalism during the year, as compared to 22 in 2015 and 23 in 2014. Graffiti swastikas continued to appear in Kyiv and other cities. On January 13, arsonists damaged a Jewish cemetery in Kolomiya, following similar attacks in 2015. On March 4, unknown persons set fire to a wreath left by the Israeli minister of justice at the Babyn Yar memorial. On April 15, vandals defaced a monument to the Holocaust in Cherkasy. In May, on Israel's national memorial day for the Holocaust, an unknown group of persons burned an Israeli flag at the Babyn Yar memorial. There were reportedly several anti-Semitic incidents targeting the memorial during the year.

Senior government officials and politicians from various political parties continued efforts to combat anti-Semitism by speaking out against extremism and social intolerance and criticizing anti-Semitic acts. On September 29, the government held a commemoration ceremony marking the 75th anniversary of the Babyn Yar massacre, during which 33,771 Jews were killed in two days during the Nazi German occupation.

Trafficking in Persons

See the Department of State's *Trafficking in Persons Report* at www.state.gov/j/tip/rls/tiprpt/.

Persons with Disabilities

The law prohibits discrimination against persons with physical, sensory, intellectual, and mental disabilities in employment, education, air travel and other transportation, access to health care, and the provision of other state services. The government did not effectively enforce these provisions.

The law requires the government to provide access to public venues and opportunities for involvement in public, educational, cultural, and sporting activities for persons with disabilities. The law also requires employers to take into account the individual needs of employees with disabilities. The government generally did not enforce these laws. According to the Ministry of Social Policy, approximately 25 percent of persons with disabilities were employed.

Advocacy groups maintained that, despite the legal requirements, most public buildings remained inaccessible to persons with disabilities, restricting the ability of such persons to participate in society. Access to employment, education, health care, transportation, and financial services remained difficult (see section 7.d.).

There were reports of societal discrimination against persons with disabilities in places of public accommodation. For example, February media reports described how a young man in Lviv, who used a wheelchair, had been repeatedly denied membership in a fitness club since 2014. The club's management gave several reasons for its refusal, including that his wheelchair could spread disease in the facility and that the man's disability could scare off other patrons.

Inclusive education remained problematic. Authorities often did not integrate students with disabilities into the general student population. Only secondary schools offered classes for students with disabilities. State employment centers lacked resources to place students with disabilities in appropriate jobs.

NGOs noted the government was unable to provide outpatient care to persons with disabilities, thus putting the main burden on their families and forcing them to place children and sometimes adults with disabilities in state institutions.

Government policy favored institutionalization of children with disabilities over placement with their families. The state cared for more than 70,000 of the country's estimated 150,000 children with disabilities, but lacked the legal framework and funds to deinstitutionalize them. Programs to provide for the basic needs of children with disabilities and inpatient and outpatient therapy programs were underfunded and understaffed. The inadequate number of educational and training programs for children with disabilities left many isolated and limited their professional opportunities in adulthood. Persons with disabilities in areas controlled by Russian-backed separatists in the east of the country suffered from a lack of appropriate care.

Patients in mental health facilities remained at risk of abuse, and many psychiatric hospitals continued to use outdated methods and medicines. According to the Ukrainian Psychiatric Association, insufficient funding, patients' lack of access to legal counsel, and poor enforcement of legal protections deprived patients with disabilities of their right to adequate medical care.

Government monitors observed incidents of involuntary seclusion and application of physical restraints to persons with mental disabilities at psychiatric and neuropsychiatric institutions of the Ministry of Social Policy. Health-care authorities placed patients in isolated and unequipped premises or even metal cages, where authorities held them for long periods without proper access to sanitation.

By law employers must set aside 4 percent of employment opportunities for persons with disabilities. NGOs noted that many of those employed to satisfy the requirement received nominal salaries but did not actually work at their companies.

On September 7, parliament adopted legislation to harmonize the country's law with international standards with respect to the rights of persons with disabilities.

National/Racial/Ethnic Minorities

Mistreatment of minority groups and harassment of foreigners of non-Slavic appearance remained problems. NGOs dedicated to combating racism and hate crimes observed that overall xenophobic incidents declined slightly during the year.

The law criminalizes deliberate actions to incite hatred or discrimination based on nationality, race, or religion, including insulting the national honor or dignity of citizens in connection with their religious and political beliefs, race, or skin color. The law imposes increased penalties for hate crimes; premeditated killing on grounds of racial, ethnic, or religious hatred carries a 10- to 15-year prison sentence. Penalties for other hate crimes include fines of 3,400 to 8,500 hryvnias ($126 to $315) or imprisonment for up to five years.

Human rights organizations stated that the requirement to prove actual intent, including proof of premeditation, to secure a conviction made application of the law difficult. Authorities did not prosecute any of the criminal proceedings under the laws on racial, national, or religious offenses. Police and prosecutors continued to prosecute racially motivated crimes under laws against hooliganism or related offenses.

According to the Prosecutor General's Office, authorities registered 58 criminal investigations involving racial, national, or religious hatred during the first nine months of the year. Of these cases 13 were closed and 15 were forwarded to court. The International Organization for Migration (IOM), reported as of October 31, 10 documented cases of violence against racial or ethnic minorities that involved 17 victims. Victims of the attacks were from Afghanistan, the Democratic Republic of the Congo, Ghana, Jordan, Nigeria, and Syria, as well as citizens of Tajik, Jewish, and Muslim descent. Most of the incidents occurred in Dnipropetrovsk, Kyiv, Kharkiv, and Odesa. There were cases of vandalism, including arson, targeting Jewish and Romani property in the Dnipropetrovsk, Cherkasy, and Zakarpattya Oblasts and in Kyiv, Lviv, Odesa, and Mykolaev.

On January 4, the Pechersk District Court in Kyiv sentenced a participant in a racist attack at a Dynamo Kyiv football match to two years in prison. Investigations into other persons involved remained open.

Roma continued to face governmental and societal discrimination. Romani rights groups estimated the Romani population at between 200,000 and 400,000. Official census data placed the number at 47,600. The discrepancy in population estimates was due in part to a lack of legal documentation for many Roma. According to experts there were more than 100 Romani NGOs, but most lacked capacity to act as effective advocates or service providers for the Romani community. Romani settlements were mainly located in the Zakarpattya, Poltava, Cherkasy, Volyn, Dnipropetrovsk, and Odesa Oblasts. Roma experienced significant barriers accessing education, health care, social services, and employment due in part to discriminatory attitudes against them.

There were reports of societal violence against Roma during the year, including cases in which police declined to intervene to stop the violence. On August 27, police failed to stop a mob from attacking a Romani settlement near Loshchynivka, Odesa Oblast, and watched while the mob vandalized Romani homes and set at least one on fire. The mob formed in reaction to the news that police arrested a man of Romani heritage in connection with the killing and rape of a local nine-year-old girl. In subsequent days local authorities announced a plan to evict Roma from their homes forcibly but cancelled the plans after the majority of recently arrived Roma fled of their own accord. Odesa's regional governor, Mikhail Saakashvili, appeared to condone the evictions, stating, "I fully share the outrage of the residents of Loshchynivka...there is massive drug-dealing in which the antisocial elements that live there are engaged. We should have fundamentally dealt with this problem earlier--and now it's simply obligatory."

There were several reports during the year that police arbitrarily detained Romani individuals, at times beating or mistreating them.

While the government in 2013 adopted a seven-year action plan to implement a strategy for protecting and integrating Roma into society, the European Roma Rights Center (ERRC) reported that it had not led to significant improvements for Roma. The ERRC monitored the plan in collaboration with the International Renaissance Foundation. According to human rights groups, the government did not allocate funds for the plan's implementation.

According to parliament's ombudsman for human rights, 24 percent of Roma have never had any schooling, and only 1 percent of the Romani population had a university degree. Approximately 31 percent of Romani children did not attend school. According to the ERRC, more than 60 percent of Roma were unemployed, creating a vicious cycle leading to social exclusion and marginalization. According to the ombudsman, securing employment was the main problem for the Romani minority. Approximately 49 percent of Roma named it as their most significant challenge.

According to the Romani women's foundation, Chiricli, local authorities erected a number of barriers to prevent issuing passports to Roma. Authorities hampered access to education for persons who lacked documents and segregated Romani children into special schools or lower-quality classrooms.

During the year many Roma fled settlements in areas controlled by Russian-backed separatists and moved elsewhere in the country. According to Chiricli approximately 10,000 Roma were among the most vulnerable members of the country's IDP community. Because many Roma lacked documents, obtaining IDP assistance, medical care, and education was especially difficult.

Acts of Violence, Discrimination, and Other Abuses Based on Sexual Orientation and Gender Identity

The labor code prohibits workplace discrimination on the basis of sexual orientation and gender identity. No law, however, prohibits such discrimination in other areas. LGBTI groups, along with international and domestic human rights organizations, criticized the lack of such language in the *National Human Rights Strategy*, although the action plan for implementation included provisions for incorporating LGBTI rights.

There was sporadic violence against LGBTI persons. For example, on February 28, hooligans assaulted two persons in Odesa after calling them a derogatory slur. While homophobic threats from right-wing nationalist groups continued, their presence at festivals and marches was often limited to several dozen counterprotesters. Although leading politicians and ministers condemned attacks on LGBTI gatherings and individuals, local officials sometimes voiced opposition to LGBTI rights and failed to protect LGBTI persons.

Overall, LGBTI groups enjoyed greater freedom to assemble than in past years. In most cases security forces and local officials deployed adequate security forces to prevent violence and protect conferences and marches. For example, security forces provided protection to an equality march in Kyiv on June 6 and a pride march in Odesa on August 11. In the case of the equality march, authorities deployed more than 6,000 security personnel, protecting more than 2,000 marchers including members of parliament. Police also adequately protected the equality festivals in Kyiv in May, in Dnipro in July, and in Zaporizhzhya in September. During an equality festival in Kyiv, right-wing groups telephoned a bomb threat. Instead of cancelling the event, security forces cleared the building, allowing the event to continue.

One notable exception was the Lviv equality festival on March 19. Hotels and conference spaces refused to honor reservations made by the festival, allegedly under pressure from city officials, who then banned all public gatherings. After the festival relocated to another hotel, security officials allowed right-wing radicals to threaten participants. After a bomb threat cancelled the conference, security forces evacuated participants on buses and took no action to prevent attacks from radicals, who threw rocks and firecrackers. Security forces failed to take action against right-wing groups that "went on safari," seeking persons suspected of being LGBTI for attack throughout the next day. According to civil society groups, assailants injured five persons after the festival.

Nash Mir LGBT Human Rights Center reported 215 instances in which persons allegedly violated the rights of LGBTI persons in the country between January and September, including 133 instances of threats and 79 instances of violence, many related to attacks in and around the Lviv equality festival. Nash Mir stated that while the number of incidents increased, there were no reports of murder or grievous harm done to LGBTI persons in the first half of the year. Crimes and discrimination against LGBTI persons remained underreported, however; and law enforcement authorities only opened 17 cases related to such acts. Nash Mir stated that extortion remained a problem and anti-LGBTI groups employed social media to entrap LGBTI persons.

Transgender persons continued to face discrimination and stereotyping in media. Medical policies towards transgendered persons improved somewhat, as, individuals no longer had to undergo sex reassignment surgery to change their names and genders officially and could do so with counseling and hormone therapy. This procedure was approved by the Ministry of Health and registered with the Ministry of Justice during the year. Regulations still prevent reassignment for married individuals and those with minor children. Transgender persons claimed to have difficulty obtaining official documents reflecting their gender.

According to Nash Mir, the situation of LGBTI persons in Russian-occupied Crimea and parts of Donetsk and Luhansk Oblasts under the control of Russian-backed separatists was very poor. Most LGBTI persons either fled or have hidden their gender identity. According to a report published by the Center for Civil Liberties and Memorial's Antidiscrimination Center in Saint Petersburg, violence and intimidation against LGBTI persons in territories controlled by Russian-backed separatists in Donetsk and Luhansk Oblasts was widespread and encouraged by Russian and Russian-backed authorities. According to the report, the Occupy Pedophilia movement was active and tolerated by local and Russian authorities. The group used social media to identify LGBTI persons and then abused them physically and verbally. According to the report, a foreign victim was beaten and forced to perform degrading acts. The report also claimed that Russian-backed separatists forced suspected LGBTI persons to dig trenches for military fortifications if ransoms were not paid.

There was overall improvement during the year in social attitudes towards homosexuality and a decline in homophobic rhetoric from churches and leading political figures, and increasing numbers of Verkhovna Rada members voiced support for LGBTI rights. Seven Verkhovna Rada members participated in the June equality march in Kyiv.

HIV and AIDS Social Stigma

UNICEF reported that children with HIV/AIDS were at high risk of abandonment, social stigma, and discrimination. Authorities prevented many children infected with HIV/AIDS from attending kindergartens or schools. They were subjected to neglect and isolated from other children. The most at-risk adolescents faced higher risk of contracting HIV/AIDs as well as additional barriers to accessing information and services for its prevention and treatment. Persons with HIV/AIDS faced discrimination and, at times, lacked access to treatment.

Section 7. Worker Rights

a. Freedom of Association and the Right to Collective Bargaining

The constitution provides for freedom of association as a fundamental right and establishes the right to participate in independent trade unions. The law also provides for the right of most workers to form and join independent unions, to bargain collectively, and to conduct legal strikes. There are no laws or legal mechanisms to prevent antiunion discrimination, although the labor code requires employers to provide justification for layoffs and firings, and union activity is not an acceptable justification. Legal recourse is available for reinstatement, back wages, and punitive damages, although observers described court enforcement as arbitrary and unpredictable, with damages too low to create incentives for compliance on the part of employers.

The law contains several limits to freedom of association and the right to collective bargaining. A number of laws that apply to worker organizations are excessively complex and contradictory. Unions reported significant bureaucratic hurdles in the registration process, entailing the payment of multiple fees and requiring visits to as many as 10 different offices. Efforts to reform legal entity registration complicated registration specifically for trade unions. Independent unions reported multiple incidents of harassment by local law enforcement officials while navigating the registration process, including nonstandard requests for documentation and membership information.

The legal procedure to initiate a strike was overly complex and effectively prohibited strike action in practice, contributing to increasing numbers of informal industrial actions. By law industrial disputes should follow procedures of consideration, conciliation, and labor arbitration that parties can draw out for months. Only after the exhaustion of this process are workers able to vote to strike, which courts may still block. The right to strike is also restricted by the requirement that a large percentage of the workforce (two-thirds of general workers' meeting delegates or 50 percent of workers in an enterprise) must vote in favor of a strike before it may be called. Poorly defined legal grounds for striking allowed the government the possibility to deny the right to strike due to national security or to protect the health or "rights and liberties" of citizens. Additionally, the law prohibits strikes by overly broad categories of workers, including personnel in the Prosecutor General's Office, the judiciary, the armed forces, the security services, law enforcement agencies, the transportation sector, and the public service sector.

In 2014 the European Court of Human Rights adjudicated restrictions in the transportation sector, declaring restrictions on strikes in the sector illegal. The decision required the government to amend legislation in conformity with the ruling, but, as of December, it had not done so. Transportation-sector workers could also refer to the Law on Transport, which regulates the strikes in the transport sector and allows strikes in case of nonfulfillment of administrative duties by employer.

Legal hurdles also made it difficult for independent unions, those not affiliated with the Federation of Trade Unions of Ukraine (FPU), to take part in tripartite negotiations, participate in social insurance programs, or represent labor at the national and international levels. These legal hurdles, set in place by outdated laws and an obsolete labor code, further entrenched the FPU and hindered the ability of smaller independent unions to act effectively when representing their members. Authorities did not enforce labor laws effectively or consistently. On the regulatory side, inspectors were limited in number and funding (also see section

7.e.). Throughout the year the labor inspection service continued to be functionally suspended due to an incomplete reorganization.

Observers disputed the independence of unions from government or employer control. Independent trade unions alleged that the country's largest trade union confederation, the FPU, enjoyed a close relationship with employers and members of some political parties. Authorities further denied unions not affiliated with the FPU a share of disputed trade union assets inherited by the FPU from Soviet-era unions, a dispute dating back more than a decade.

Statutory worker-management commissions were not always effective. Management at times dominated the commissions. There were cases where workers who renounced membership in an FPU-affiliated union and joined an independent union faced loss of pay, undesirable work assignments, and dismissal.

Several pieces of legislation passed during the year weakened protection of freedom of association, including the aforementioned law complicating trade union registration and a law complicating the tax status of trade unions.

Independent union representatives continued to be subjected to violence and intimidation. In January the deputy head of the Kryvyi Rih, Dnipropetrovsk chapter of the Independent Trade Union of Miners of Ukraine (NPGU), Elena Maslova, was beaten on her way home from work. NPGU president, Mykhaylo Volinets, claimed the attack was in response to Maslova's union activities. The union reported that authorities have not identified any perpetrators and did not investigate the attack.

In February the president of the Novovolinsk chapter of the NPGU, Anatoliy Muhomedzhanov, was beaten in the office of the mine's director. The trade union alleged that multiple witnesses saw who beat him, but police did not pursue the incident.

Arrears and corruption issues exacerbated industrial relations and led to numerous protests. In August the NPGU leader in Selidovo and Novogrodifka, Victor Trifonov, set himself on fire during a sit-in in the Kyiv building of the Ministry of Energy and Coal of Ukraine. In response government officials accused trade union members of siding with separatists in the east of the country.

In September the president of the Free Health-care Workers Union, Oleg Panasenko, reported that unknown persons destroyed a union protest camp at the entrance of the Ministry of Health, while police were present and failed to intervene.

b. Prohibition of Forced or Compulsory Labor

The law prohibits all forms of forced or compulsory labor. Penalties for violations ranged from three to 15 years imprisonment and were sufficiently stringent to deter violations, but resources, inspections, and remediation were inadequate to provide for enforcement. In the first nine months of the year, the IOM assisted 777 victims of trafficking in the country: 312 women and 465 men. Approximately 93 percent of the victims had been subjected to labor exploitation.

There were reports of trafficking of women, men, and children for labor. Traffickers subjected some foreign nationals to forced labor in construction, agriculture, manufacturing, domestic work, the lumber industry, nursing, and street begging. Traffickers subjected some children to forced labor (see section 7.c.) The government made minor efforts to prevent or eliminate forced labor, citing a lack of budgetary resources.

According to the IOM, identified victims of trafficking received comprehensive reintegration assistance, including legal aid, medical care, psychological counseling, financial support, vocational training, and other types of assistance based on individual needs.

Also, see the Department of State's *Trafficking in Persons Report* at www.state.gov/j/tip/rls/tiprpt/.

c. Prohibition of Child Labor and Minimum Age for Employment

The law sets 16 as the minimum age for most employment. Children who are 15 years of age may perform undefined "light work" with a parent's consent, leaving the issue open to interpretation by employers and opening the system to abuse. The law allows children to do some forms of "nonhazardous" work beginning at 14 as part of an apprenticeship in the context of vocational training.

The government did not effectively enforce the law due to a lack of resources within the Ministry of Social Policy and a continued moratorium on surprise labor inspections for much of the year. Penalties for violations ranged from small fines for illegitimate employment or other labor law violations to prison sentences for sexual exploitation of a child or involvement of a child in illicit activities or pornography; they were insufficient to deter violations. The penalty for forcing children to beg is imprisonment for up to three years.

The most frequent violations of child labor laws related to work in hazardous conditions, long workdays, failure to maintain work records, and delayed salary payments.

As of September 20, the territorial bodies of the State Service on Labor had conducted 2,547 inspections in which they examined compliance with child labor laws. The inspections found 112 instances of the use of child labor and 105 violations of the law. The businesses inspected included 17 agricultural enterprises, 24 trade companies, 35 service providers, and 36 companies in other sectors. The inspections uncovered 252 working minors, of whom 56 were 14 to 15 years old and 196 were 16 to 18 years old.

There were reports of child soldiers among the Russian-backed separatist forces in the east of the country (see section 1.g., Child Soldiers).

Also see the Department of Labor's *Findings on the Worst Forms of Child Labor* at www.dol.gov/ilab/reports/child-labor/findings/.

d. Discrimination with Respect to Employment and Occupation

The labor code prohibits discrimination in the workplace based on race, color, political, religious and other beliefs, sex, gender identity, sexual orientation, ethnic, social, and foreign origin, age, health, disability, HIV/AIDS condition, family and property status, or linguistic or other grounds.

The government did not effectively enforce the law, and discrimination in employment and occupation reportedly occurred with respect to gender, disability, nationality, race, minority status, sexual orientation or gender identity, and HIV-positive status. The agriculture, construction, mining, heavy industry, and services sectors had the most work-related discrimination. The law provides for civil, administrative, and criminal liability for discrimination in the workplace. Penalties include a fine of up to 50 tax-free minimum incomes, correctional labor for a term of up to two years or restraint of liberty for a term up to five years, with or without the deprivation of the right to occupy certain positions or engage in certain activities for a term up to three years. Such actions accompanied by violence, are punishable by correctional labor for a term of up to two years, imprisonment for a term of up to five years, or imprisonment for a term of two to five years, if such actions were committed by an organized group of persons or if they caused death or other grave consequences.

Industries dominated by female workers had the lowest relative wages. Women received lower salaries due to limited opportunities for advancement and the types of industries that employed them. According to the Human Rights Ombudsman's Office, men earned on average 29.5 percent more than women. Domestic and international observers noted that women held few elected or appointed offices at the national and regional levels. Additionally, the law limits women's employment opportunities and prohibits women from engaging in more than 500 occupations, including bulldozer operator and bus driver.

e. Acceptable Conditions of Work

The monthly minimum wage was 1,378 hryvnias ($51) from January 1 through April 30; it rose to 1,450 hryvnias ($54) on May 1 and to 1,600 hryvnias ($59) on December 1. As of January 1, 2017, the minimum wage for private-sector workers is to increase to 3,200 hryvnias ($119) according to the 2017 draft budget. The hourly minimum wage was 8.29 hryvnias ($0.31) from January through April and rose to 8.69 hryvnias ($0.32) on May 1 and to 9.29 hryvnias $.034) on December 1. Some workers in the informal sector received wages below the established minimum. The poverty income level rose during the year from 1,330 hryvnias ($49) per month to 1,399 hryvnias ($52) during the year.

The labor law provides for a maximum 40-hour workweek, with a minimum 42-hour period of rest per week and at least 24 days of paid vacation per year. It provides for double pay for overtime work and regulates the number of overtime hours allowed. The law requires agreement between employers and the respective local trade union organization on all overtime work and limits overtime to four hours during two consecutive days and 120 hours per year.

Wage arrears continued to be a major problem during the year. A lack of legal remedies, bureaucratic wrangling, and corruption in public and private enterprises, often blocked efforts to recover overdue wages, leading to significant wage theft.

In July the NPGU reported that arrears in the coal sector reached almost 496 million hryvnias ($18.4 million). Arrears and corruption issues exacerbated industrial relations and led to numerous protests.

Total wage arrears in the country rose during the year to 1.9 billion hryvnias ($70 million) as of September 1. More than half of the debt was in the Luhansk (23.2 percent), Donetsk, (19.6 percent), and Kharkiv (10.1 percent) regions.

The law requires employers to provide safe workplaces. While the law and associated regulations contain occupational safety and health standards, employers frequently ignored them due to the lack of enforcement mechanisms and the government's failure to hold employers accountable for unsafe conditions. The law provides workers the right to remove themselves from dangerous working conditions without jeopardizing their continued employment. According to one NGO, employers in the metal and mining industries often violated the rule and retaliated against workers by pressuring them to quit.

Penalties for violations ranged from 510 to 1,700 hryvnias ($19 to $63), which were insufficient to deter violations. The State Labor Inspectorate was responsible for enforcing labor laws. Inspectors were limited in number and funding. By 2014, the latest date for which such data were available, the number of inspectors had dropped to 457 from 616, in large part due to a 70 percent funding cut that year.

The government did not effectively enforce minimum wage, hours of work, and occupational safety and health standards in all sectors, including the informal economy. Penalties for violations included fines of 50 to 100 tax-free minimum incomes, limitations on the right to occupy positions of responsibility or to engage in some activities for three to five years, correctional labor for up to two years, or arrest for up to six months if the actions committed affected a minor or a pregnant woman. It is impossible to determine whether these penalties were enough to deter violations as with little to no inspection regime, coupled with a largely nonfunctioning reporting mechanism, it was difficult for the government to detect violations. The government has had a moratorium in place on surprise inspections since 2014, with the goal of cutting the number of required inspections and certifications, deregulating the economy, and preventing corruption. The moratorium constrained the government's ability to enforce labor laws effectively. During this period authorities required the State Labor Service and its predecessor, the State Labor Inspectorate, to pursue a lengthy interagency process to obtain permission from the Cabinet of Ministers to conduct an inspection. Labor inspections could also occur at a company's request or upon the formal request of the investigator in the framework of criminal proceedings against a company.

Lax safety standards and aging equipment caused many injuries on the job. Wage arrears, nonpayment of overtime, operational safety problems, and health complaints were common in the mining industry.

Mineworkers, particularly in the illegal mining sector, faced very serious safety and health problems. Through September there were 144 incidents resulting in mining injuries, including 17 fatalities, or approximately 8 percent fewer injuries but 54 percent more fatalities than in the same period in 2015. During the same period, authorities reported 635 individual injuries to coal miners, or almost 17 percent above the same period in 2015. Also through September there were 3,168 occupational injuries for all employment types (including 298 fatalities), which was 0.5 percent (11 percent) above the same period in 2015. Workers faced unsafe situations in areas outside government control in the Donetsk and Luhansk Oblasts.

Despite Russian aggression close to industrial areas in the Donbas region, enterprises involved in mining, energy, media, retail, clay production, and transportation continued to operate through December. Fighting resulted in physical damage to mines and plants through loss of power, destroyed transformers, physical damage from shelling, and reportedly intentional flooding of mines by combined Russian-separatist forces. Miners were especially vulnerable, as loss of electrical power could strand them underground. Additionally, loss of electrical power threatened the operability of mine safety equipment that prevented the buildup of explosive gases.

CRIMEA

In February 2014 Russian forces entered Ukraine's Crimean Peninsula and occupied it militarily. In March 2014 Russia announced the peninsula had become part of the Russian Federation following a sham referendum that violated Ukraine's constitution. On March 27, 2014, the UN General Assembly adopted Resolution 68/262 on the "Territorial Integrity of Ukraine," which called on states and international organizations not to recognize any change in Crimea's status and affirmed the commitment of the UN to recognize Crimea as part of Ukraine. In April 2014 Ukraine's legislature (Verkhovna Rada) adopted a law attributing responsibility for human rights violations in Crimea to the Russian Federation as the occupying state. The United States does not recognize the attempted "annexation" of Crimea by the Russian Federation. Russian law has de facto applied in Ukraine's Crimea since the Russian occupation and purported "annexation" of the peninsula. For detailed information on the laws and practices of the Russian Federation, see the Country Reports on Human Rights for Russia.

EXECUTIVE SUMMARY

A local authority installed by the Russian government and led by Sergey Aksyonov as "prime minister" of the "state council of the republic of Crimea" administered occupied Crimea. The "state council" was responsible for day-to-day administration and other functions of governing. On September 18, Russia's nationwide parliamentary elections included seats allocated for occupied Crimea, a move widely condemned by the international community. "Authorities" closed the election to independent observers; it was not free and fair and was held in contravention of the Ukrainian constitution.

Russian authorities maintained control over Russian military and security forces deployed in Crimea.

Russian security services continued to consolidate control over Crimea and restrict human rights. Occupation authorities imposed and disproportionately applied repressive Russian Federation laws on the Ukrainian territory of Crimea.

The most significant human rights problems in Crimea during the year related directly to the Russian occupation.

Russian security services engaged in an extensive campaign of intimidation to suppress dissent and opposition to the occupation that employed kidnappings, disappearances, physical abuse, political prosecution, repeated interviews, and interrogations by security forces. Russian security forces routinely detained individuals without cause and harassed and intimidated neighbors and family of those who opposed the occupation.

Occupation authorities deprived members of certain groups, particularly ethnic Ukrainians and Crimean Tatars, of fundamental civil liberties, including the freedom to express their nationality and ethnicity, subjecting them to systematic discrimination. On May 12, Russian authorities banned the Crimean Tatar Mejlis, a democratically elected body representing the Crimean Tatar people, claiming it was an extremist organization, and prohibited all meetings, gatherings, or financial activities of the group. Continuing their policy of imposing Russian citizenship on all residents of Crimea, occupation authorities subjected persons who refused Russian citizenship to discrimination in accessing education, health care, and employment. They also interfered with freedom of expression and assembly, criminalizing the display of cultural and national symbols, preventing groups of private individuals from celebrating their national and cultural heritage, and restricting access to education in Ukrainian and Crimean Tatar languages.

Russian authorities engaged in a widespread campaign to suppress free speech and media in Crimea. Independent media ceased to operate in Crimea. Occupation authorities questioned, detained, and charged with extremism the few remaining independent journalists who worked independently, often merely for expressing their belief that Crimea remained part of Ukraine.

Other problems included poor conditions in prisons and pretrial detention facilities; political interference in the judicial process; limitations on freedom of movement; the internal displacement of thousands of individuals to government-controlled Ukraine; failure to allow residents of Ukraine's region of Crimea to exercise the ability to vote in periodic and genuine elections to choose their leaders; official corruption; discrimination and abuse of ethnic and religious minority groups; discrimination against lesbian, gay, bisexual, transgender, and intersex (LGBTI) persons; kidnapping and transport of orphans to Russia by occupation authorities; and employment discrimination against persons who did not hold a Russian passport.

Russian-installed authorities took few steps to investigate or prosecute officials or individuals who committed human rights abuses, creating an atmosphere of impunity and lawlessness. Occupation and local "self-defense" forces often did not wear insignia and committed abuses with impunity.

Section 1. Respect for the Integrity of the Person, Including Freedom from:

a. Arbitrary Deprivation of Life and other Unlawful or Politically Motivated Killings

Russian occupation authorities did not adequately investigate cases of abductions and killings of Crimean residents from 2014 and 2015. According to the Ukrainian Ministry of Foreign Affairs, 12 Crimean residents who had disappeared during the occupation were later found dead. Occupation authorities did not investigate other suspicious deaths and disappearances, occasionally categorizing them as suicide. Human rights observers reported that families frequently did not challenge findings in such cases due to fear of retaliation.

b. Disappearance

According to the Ukrainian Ministry of Foreign Affairs and the Crimean Tatar Mejlis, as of October 1, 28 persons had disappeared since the occupation of Crimea, including 12 later found dead. Russian occupation authorities did not adequately investigate the deaths and disappearances. Human rights groups reported that police often refused to register reports of disappearances and intimidated and threatened with detention those who tried to report a disappearance. Ukrainian government and human rights groups believed Russian security forces kidnapped the individuals for opposing Russia's occupation to instill fear in the population and prevent dissent.

On May 24, a group of uniformed men kidnapped Ervin Ibragimov, a member of the Bakhchisaray Mejlis and of the Coordinating Council of the World Congress of Crimean Tatars, after stopping his car on a road outside Bakhchisaray. Footage from a closed-circuit television camera showed the men forcing Ibragimov into a car and departing. According to the Crimea Human Rights Group, the men wore uniforms of the Ministry of Internal Affairs' traffic police. According to the HRMMU, on May 25, Ibragimov's father went to the Federal Security Service (FSB) in Simferopol to file a complaint and provide the television footage. The FSB officers allegedly refused to file the complaint and told him to send it by mail. A week before he disappeared, Ibragimov told friends that he had noticed a car waiting outside his house that later followed him during the day. Ibragimov had planned to travel to the town of Sudak on May 25 to attend the court hearing of a group of Crimean Tatars charged for holding an "unauthorized" gathering on May 18 to mark Crimean Tatar Deportation Remembrance Day. On June 1, Ibragimov's employment record book and passport were found near a bar in Bakhchisaray. While occupation authorities opened an investigation into the case, according to the Crimea Human Rights Group, they specifically excluded the possibility of a political motivation for the disappearance or of state involvement.

c. Torture and Other Cruel, Inhuman, or Degrading Treatment or Punishment

There were widespread reports that Russian authorities in Crimea abused residents who opposed the occupation. Human rights monitors reported that Russian occupying forces subjected Crimean Tatars and ethnic Ukrainians in particular to physical abuse. For example, on June 11, Ukrainian blogger and activist, Yuri Ilchenko, escaped from house arrest in Sevastopol and fled across the administrative boundary to government-controlled Ukraine. Ilchenko had been awaiting trial on extremism charges from February 2015 for his online writings expressing his opposition to the occupation of Crimea. Ilchenko and his parents claimed to be the first individuals in Sevastopol formally to decline taking Russian citizenship. In August he gave several accounts to the press describing his mistreatment during detention in a pretrial facility in Simferopol that lasted from February 2015 through June 2. Ilchenko claimed that security officials had repeatedly beaten him and collaborated with other inmates to continue beatings and threats while he was in detention, to coerce him explicitly into taking Russian citizenship, and to punish him for speaking Ukrainian. He claimed they forced him to remain awake for days and beat him when he fell asleep in retaliation for refusing to wear a "St. George's ribbon," a Russian military symbol. Ilchenko claimed occupation authorities denied him clothing, bedding, and medical care.

Occupation authorities demonstrated a pattern of using punitive psychiatric incarceration as a means of pressuring detained individuals, including in the case of Ilmi Umerov (see section 1.d.). For example, on November 3, authorities ordered that six Crimean Tatar defendants accused of belonging to Hizb-ut-Tahrir be subjected to psychiatric evaluation and confinement against their will without apparent medical need (see section 1.d.).

Human rights monitors reported that occupation authorities also threatened individuals with violence or imprisonment if they did not testify in court against individuals that authorities believed were opposed to the occupation.

Prison and Detention Center Conditions

<u>Physical Conditions</u>: Prison and detention center conditions reportedly remained harsh and overcrowded. In June the director of the Russian Federal Prison System stated that Crimea lacked sufficient prison facilities and that there were twice as many inmates as there were cells necessary to house them. Human rights groups reported that prisons suffered from overcrowding and poor conditions.

According to a 2015 report on Crimea by the OSCE's Office of Democratic Institutions and Human Rights (ODIHR) and the OSCE High Commissioner on National Minorities, health care in prisons had deteriorated since the occupation began. Yuri Ilchenko reported that prisoners in the Simferopol pretrial detention facility lacked proper food, sanitation, and health care. On March 1, the Crimea Human Rights Group reported that a group of four Crimean Tatars detained in February on politically motivated "terrorism" charges were living in cells in a Simferopol pretrial facility that were infested with fleas and bedbugs, were forced to sleep in shifts on a single filthy bed, and given food that contained cockroaches.

<u>Administration</u>: According to the 2015 OSCE/ODIHR report, persons incarcerated during the Russian occupation did not have the opportunity to retain Ukrainian citizenship. Russian authorities compelled all individuals who were in prison or pretrial facilities when the occupation began to accept Russian citizenship. As of August the Human Rights Ombudsman's Offices of Ukraine and Russia were working on a solution that would allow some prisoners to return to Ukraine.

<u>Independent Monitoring</u>: Occupation authorities did not permit monitoring of prison or detention center conditions by independent nongovernmental observers or international organizations. Occupation authorities permitted "human rights ombudsman," Ludmila Lubina, to visit prisoners, but human rights activists regarded Lubina not as an independent actor but as representing the interests of the occupation authorities.

d. Arbitrary Arrest or Detention

Occupation authorities arbitrarily detained protesters, activists, and journalists for opposing the Russian occupation.

Role of the Police and Security Apparatus

Russian government agencies, including the Ministry of Internal Affairs, the FSB, the Federal Investigative Committee, and the Office of the Prosecutor General applied and enforced Russian law in Crimea. The FSB also conducted security, counterintelligence, and counterterrorism activities and combatted organized crime and corruption. A "national police force" operated under the aegis of the Russian Ministry of Internal Affairs.

In addition to abuses committed by Russian forces, "self-defense forces," largely consisting of former Ukrainian Ministry of Interior officers allegedly linked to local organized crime, reportedly continued to operate and commit abuses. These forces often acted with impunity in intimidating perceived occupation opponents and were involved in extrajudicial detentions and arbitrary confiscation of property. While the "law" places the "self-defense forces" under the authority of the "national police," their members continued to commit abuses while receiving state funding for their activities as well as other rewards, such as beachfront property and service medals. For example, on December 8, members of "self-defense" forces allegedly beat two residents of the village of Shchelkino. Police arriving at the scene declined to arrest members of the self-defense forces. An investigation into the incident continued.

Arrest Procedures and Treatment of Detainees

<u>Arbitrary Arrest</u>: There were reports that Russian occupation authorities made arbitrary arrests, in particular targeting Crimean Tatars.

On May 12, police arrested Ilmi Umerov, a member of the Crimean Tatar Mejlis, accusing him of "undermining the territorial integrity of the Russian Federation" for stating that Crimea remains part of Ukraine. Umerov, who suffered from health problems, has since been taken from court hearings in poor health. On August 18, Umerov was forcibly subjected to psychiatric hospitalization, ostensibly for an examination, exacerbating his health problems. On September 7, occupation authorities released him from the hospital following international publicity over the case. At year's end his case remained in pretrial investigation.

As of October 25, occupation authorities had arrested 19 Crimean residents, mostly Crimean Tatars, accusing them of belonging to Hizb-ut-Tahrir, a pan-Islamic organization prohibited in Russia but not Ukraine. Human rights groups believed occupation authorities intended to intimidate Crimean Tatars, discredit the Mejlis leadership, and instill fear in the local population to prevent dissent through the arrests.

Russian authorities continued to detain Akhtem Chiygoz, the deputy leader of the Crimean Tatar Mejlis. Russian authorities arrested Chiygoz in January 2015 and charged him with "inciting a mass riot" during protests he organized at the Crimean parliament in 2014 that were disrupted by pro-Russian activists, resulting in clashes between the groups. Subsequently, occupation authorities prosecuted individuals alleged to have participated in the protest, although Russia did not exercise control over Crimea at the time. Human rights groups reported that authorities reviewed video of the incident and selectively brought charges against leading Crimean Tatar and Ukrainian individuals who subsequently opposed the occupation, in particular members of the Crimean Tatar Mejlis. Video footage shows Chiygoz and other Crimean Tatar leaders working to defuse tensions in the hopes of avoiding clashes with counterprotesters. Occupation authorities refused to investigate acts of violence committed by pro-Russian "protesters," who were likely working for Russian security services according to independent observers. On December 12, authorities extended Chiygoz's detention until April 2017.

Throughout the year Russian authorities conducted mass arrests designed to humiliate and intimidate Crimean Tatars. On April 1, Russian security forces detained 35 men, mostly Crimean Tatars, in Pionierske, took them to a "center to combat extremism," and collected DNA samples from them. Human rights groups claimed that Russian security forces attempted to recruit some as police informants. On May 6, Russian security forces detained more than 100 Crimean Tatars at a mosque in Molodizhne. On May 7, Russian security forces detained another 35 Muslims, many of whom were Crimean Tatars, at a market in Simferopol.

e. Denial of Fair Public Trial

Under the Russian occupation regime, the "judiciary" was neither independent nor impartial.

Trial Procedures

See the *Country Reports on Human Rights* for Russia for a description of the relevant Russian laws and procedures that the Russian government applied and enforced in occupied Crimea.

Political Prisoners and Detainees

Russian occupation authorities routinely detained and prosecuted individuals for political reasons (see section 1.d.). They also transferred Crimean cases to Russia's legal system and changed the venue of prosecution for some detainees. Human rights groups identified several dozen Crimean residents as political prisoners held in either Crimea or Russia. These included: Oleg Sentsov, Oleksander Kolchenko, Oleksiy Chirniy, Oleksander Kostenko, Ilmi Umerov, Akhtem Chiygoz, Ali Asanov, Mustafa Dehermedzhy, Mykola Semena, Andrii Kolomiets, Ruslan Zaytullaev, Rustam Vaytov, Nuri Primov, Ferat Sayfullaev, Enver Bekirov, Vadim Siruk, Muslim Aliev, Emir-Ussein Kuku, Refat Alimov, Arcen Dzhepparov, Enver Mamutov, Remzi Memetov, Zevri Abseitov, Rustem Abultarov, and others.

According to Mejlis member Gayana Yuksel, as of October 26, occupation authorities have deprived 67 Crimean Tatar children of a parent because of politically motivated imprisonment since the start of the occupation.

f. Arbitrary or Unlawful Interference with Privacy, Family, Home, or Correspondence

Occupation authorities and others engaged in electronic surveillance, entered residences and other premises without warrants, and harassed relatives and neighbors of perceived opposition figures.

Russian occupation authorities routinely conducted raids on homes to intimidate the local population, particularly Crimean Tatars and ethnic Ukrainians, ostensibly on the grounds of searching for weapons, drugs, or "extremist literature." In its June report, the HRMMU expressed concern about "the growing number of large scale 'police' actions conducted with the apparent intention to harass and intimidate Crimean Tatars and other Muslim believers." On February 11 and 12, Russian occupation authorities raided Crimean Tatar villages in the Yalta and Bakhchisaray regions. According to the Crimea Human Rights Group, men with guns and in balaclavas burst into homes and in some cases broke through doors or windows, despite encountering no resistance from the residents. Between April 16 and 20, authorities conducted several raids on Crimean Tatar homes in the Alyushta region. According to press reports, police entered Crimean Tatar homes and demanded to know how many persons lived in the house, where they went shopping, where their children studied, and who sold drugs in the village. They also demanded to inspect gardens and greenhouses.

Human rights groups reported that Russian authorities had widespread authority to tap telephones and read electronic communications and had established a network of informants to report on suspicious activities. According to Mejlis members, Russian authorities had invited hundreds of Crimean Tatars to "interviews" where authorities played back the interviewees' telephone conversations and read their e-mail aloud. Media reported that in July the FSB interviewed a doctor in a Feodosia hospital after a colleague had denounced him for privately expressing pro-Ukrainian views. The doctor stated that posters in the hospital hallways advertised an FSB hotline. The eavesdropping and visits by security personnel create an environment in which persons are afraid to voice any opinion contrary to the occupation authorities, even in private.

According to press reports, on January 22, the Russian FSB sent a notice to all post offices in Crimea containing a list of individuals deemed "extremist," but which was in fact a list of individuals known to oppose the occupation, with instructions to report to the FSB any correspondence sent or received by these individuals.

Occupation authorities harassed family members of a number of political opponents. On February 2, Russian migration and security officials questioned Erol Abdulzhelilov, grandson of Crimean Tatar leader Mustafa Jemilev, demanding his passport and summoning him to a police station. On February 18, Russian authorities summoned Yevgeny Kostenko, the brother of Oleksander Kostenko, imprisoned on political grounds, and threatened him with a forced psychiatric examination when he refused to answer questions. On September 26, occupation authorities pressured the young children of imprisoned Crimean Tatar activist, Emir-Ussein Kuku, to make statements about Kuku that could be used to strip him of his parental rights.

Following the sabotage of electrical lines from government-controlled territory to occupied Crimea, Russian officials cut power and natural gas to the homes of Crimean Tatar Mejlis members in retaliation.

Section 2. Respect for Civil Liberties, Including:

a. Freedom of Speech and Press

Occupation authorities significantly restricted freedom of speech and press, and subjected dissenting voices to harassment and prosecution. They refused to register independent print and broadcast media outlets, forcing them to cease operations. Threats and harassment against international and Ukrainian journalists were common.

Freedom of Speech and Expression: Individuals could not publicly criticize the Russian occupation without fear of reprisal. Human rights groups reported that the FSB engaged in widespread surveillance of social media, telephones, and electronic communication and routinely summoned individuals for "discussions" for voicing or posting opposition to the Russian occupation.

For example, on August 12, occupation authorities in Yalta charged Larysa Kitaiska with extremism because of a social media posting that they believed to be anti-Russian. Kitaiska had left Crimea for mainland Ukraine after the occupation began, but had temporarily returned to resolve a property matter when she was charged. Kitaiska left Crimea shortly after she was charged; she maintained that occupation authorities brought the case in retaliation for her pro-Ukrainian views and participation in the 2013-14 Euromaidan movement.

On October 5, armed security forces raided the home of Suleyman Kadyrov, a member of the Feodosia Mejlis, because of a March Facebook posting in which Kadyrov stated that Crimea remains a part of Ukraine. On October 11, occupation authorities charged Kadyrov with separatism.

<u>Press and Media Freedoms</u>: Independent print and broadcast media could not operate freely. Occupation authorities refused to register most independent media outlets, forcing them to close in 2015.

On March 25, *Krymska Svitlytsya*, the only Ukrainian-language newspaper remaining in Crimea, ceased publication. According to its website, the newspaper moved operations to Kyiv after it could no longer provide for the safety of its employees in Crimea.

On January 15, Russian occupation forces detained blogger and journalist Zair Akadyrov as he covered the trial of the "February 26" group of political prisoners and took him to a police precinct for questioning.

On December 7, the "prosecutor general" of Crimea charged Mykola Semena with "undermining Russian territorial integrity via mass media," a criminal offense punishable up to five years in prison. Semena, a freelance writer for the news website *Krym Realii*, had written pieces using a pseudonym criticizing the de facto Crimean government and Russian occupation. Occupation authorities detained Semena twice in 2015, and human rights groups believed that Russian security forces hacked into his computer to prove he had written articles critical of the occupation. Authorities placed Semena, who was in poor health, under house arrest in April, under the condition that he not leave Crimea. On September 29, a judge denied Semena's request to seek medical treatment in government-controlled Ukraine.

On June 14, Russian occupation authorities arrested Alexi Sapov, editor of *Argumenty Nedeli-Krym*. Sapov was one of the last reporters to cover the trials of Crimean Tatars. Sapov was previously a journalist in Vladimir, Russia, where his reporting led to accusations that he had blackmailed a member of the Russian parliament. Russian authorities extradited Sapov to Vladimir, Russia.

<u>Violence and Harassment</u>: There were numerous cases of Russian security forces or police harassing independent media and detaining journalists in connection with their professional activities.

On May 11, Russian authorities detained Igor Burdyga, a Ukrainian journalist covering the anniversary of the deportation of Crimean Tatars. According to Burdyga authorities detained him for his journalistic work, accused him of being a member of the Ukrainian nationalist group Right Sector, and forced him to testify that he had been involved in the demolition of electrical power lines in Ukraine that supplied Crimea. After seven hours of detention, authorities released Burdyga and he left Crimea.

Censorship or Content Restrictions: Following Russia's occupation of Crimea, journalists overwhelmingly resorted to self-censorship to continue reporting and broadcasting. Russian occupation authorities banned most Ukrainian and Crimean Tatar-language broadcasts, replacing the content with Russian programming. Human rights groups reported that Russian authorities forbade songs by Ukrainian singers, such as Ruslana and Jamala, from playing on Crimean radio stations. Censorship of independent internet sites became more widespread.

Internet Freedom

Russian occupation authorities restricted free expression on the internet by imposing repressive laws of the Russian Federation on Crimea (see section 2.a. of the *Country Reports on Human Rights* for Russia). Security services routinely monitored and controlled internet activity to suppress contrary opinions. According to media accounts, occupation authorities interrogated residents of Crimea for posting pro-Ukrainian opinions on Facebook or in blogs.

On May 27, journalist Lilia Bujurova received a warning from security forces about postings she made on social media that Crimea was part of Ukraine.

On November 11, the Yevpatoria city court sentenced Serhiy Vasylchenko, a local anarchist, to 10 days in jail for "extremism" after he made calls on social media to boycott the Russian Duma elections in Crimea.

Throughout the year, Russian authorities blocked internet sites they considered "extremist," but that in fact provided mainstream reporting about the situation in Crimea. For example, in February they blocked the sites of *Ukrainska Pravda*, *censor.net*, and *Apostrophe*. Following the arrest of Mykola Semena in April, Russian authorities blocked the website of *Krym Realii*. By August Russian authorities had blocked more than 60 websites as "extremist" for stating that Crimea remained a part of Ukraine.

Academic Freedom and Cultural Events

Russian authorities in Crimea engaged in a widespread campaign to suppress Crimean Tatar and Ukrainian languages. While Crimean Tatar and Ukrainian are official languages in occupied Crimea, authorities continued to reduce instruction in schools and offered the languages only as an optional language at the end of the school day. In 2015 authorities closed the Crimean Tatar school in Bakhchysarai. The Mejlis reported that authorities continued to pressure Crimean Tatars to use the Cyrillic, as opposed to the Latin, alphabet.

On May 27, Russian security officers interviewed children at School No. 15 in Blizhne, Feodosia District, after receiving reports that some had not worn the St. George's Ribbon, a Russian military symbol, on May 9. According to human rights monitors, authorities interviewed students about their opinions on Ukrainian sovereignty over Crimea. Authorities singled out Crimean Tatar boys for questioning, and witnesses reported that FSB officers stated they would conduct similar investigations in the future.

b. Freedom of Peaceful Assembly and Association

Freedom of Assembly

Organizations representing minority communities reported gross and widespread harassment and intimidation by occupation authorities to suppress their ability to assemble peacefully. Abuses included arbitrary searches, interrogations, threats of deportation, and unsubstantiated accusations of possessing "extremist" literature.

According to the HRMMU, on July 4, occupation authorities amended a 2014 resolution listing the places in Crimea where public events could be held, decreasing the number almost by half (from 665 to 366). The HRMMU noted that the amendments further restricted freedom of assembly to a shrinking number of "specially designated spaces," an unnecessary move that appeared "designed to dissuade the exercise of the right of freedom of assembly."

On March 1, authorities in Simferopol refused to allow the commemoration of the birthdate of Taras Shevchenko, the national poet of Ukraine. On March 9, Simferopol authorities issued a blanket prohibition on public gatherings not organized by the government from March 7 to March 22.

Occupation authorities prohibited gatherings and meetings to commemorate the 72nd anniversary of the 1944 Soviet mass deportation of Crimean Tatars on May 18. On May 17, Ilmi Umerov received a preemptive warning from police not to organize any type of gathering. In the days leading up to the anniversary, schoolteachers forbade students, particularly Crimean Tatar students, to skip school to participate in commemorative events. The Mejlis reported that Crimean Tatar communities did not seek permission for gatherings as they assumed that occupation authorities would forbid them. Throughout Crimea peaceful assemblies took place, but authorities arrested Crimean Tatars displaying flags and other symbols, including at least one person in Bakhchysarai, four in the Kirovsky District, and four in Sudak.

Occupation authorities forbade any assembly marking Crimean Tatar Flag Day on June 26.

On August 20, a group named The Deceived of Crimea gathered in Simferopol to protest rampant corruption in Crimea following Russia's occupation in 2014. Despite having obtained permission from the local government, authorities prohibited protesters from assembling for a demonstration planned to coincide with a visit by President Putin of Russia.

There were reports of occupation authorities using coercive methods to provide for participation at pro-"government" rallies. For example, according to press reports, a Duma candidate shared on social media a photograph of an order authorities sent to municipal government offices in Feodosia, which stated that attendance at a September 8 rally in support of the United Russia party was mandatory and that those unable to attend must write an explanatory note to their superiors.

There were reports that occupation authorities charged and fined individuals for allegedly violating public assembly rules in retaliation for gathering to witness security force raids on homes. For example, courts fined at least five Crimean Tatars for gathering to witness security force raids on neighboring homes in Bakhchisarai in May. Crimean Tatar leaders claim the charges were designed to intimidate Crimean Tatars into passively remaining in their homes during raids.

Freedom of Association

Occupation authorities broadly restricted freedom of association for individuals that opposed the occupation.

On February 15, the "prosecutor general" of Crimea filed a motion to ban the Crimean Tatar Mejlis, an elected, representative body of Crimean Tatars that the Ukrainian government legally recognizes. On April 13, the prosecutor general provisionally banned the Mejlis pending a court decision; the Russian Ministry of Justice upheld the decision on April 18. On April 26, a Russian occupation court declared the Mejlis an extremist organization for continuing to recognize Ukrainian sovereignty in Crimea. On September 29, the Russian Supreme Court upheld the lower court's decision. The ban forbids Mejlis organized meetings or demonstrations, sharply restricts its financial activities, and prohibits the display of the Mejlis flag and symbols. While the Mejlis was led by a central council of 33 members, its organization extended to towns and villages, meaning that up to 2,000 local members of Mejlis groups were under threat.

In late September authorities fined at least eight Mejlis members for allegedly taking part in a meeting of an illegal organization, stemming from their informal gathering at the home of Ilmi Umerov on September 22. They had gathered to wish exiled Crimean Tatar leader, Refat Chubarov, a happy birthday via Skype, but authorities had monitored the meeting and determined that it constituted a meeting of the banned Mejlis. On December 29, Umerov announced that he was unable to pay the fine as occupation authorities had frozen his bank accounts by putting him on a list of "extremists."

On February 11, Russian authorities summoned Nariman Jelal, the highest ranking member of the Crimean Tatar Mejlis not incarcerated or exiled, demanding he detail the activities of the Crimean Tatar Mejlis and his future travel plans.

Russian authorities raided groups and institutions associated with Ukrainian culture. On March 31, security forces raided the Taras Shevchenko Association in Simferopol and seized approximately 250 books for promoting Ukrainian nationalism. Many of the seized materials dealt with the Holodomor, a famine produced by Soviet authorities in 1932 and 1933 that led to the deaths of millions of Ukrainians. On July 18, authorities questioned Leonid Kuzmin, a member of the Ukrainian Cultural Association. Authorities compelled Kuzmin to sign a nondisclosure agreement, forbidding discussion of the grounds for his questioning.

Russian occupation authorities carried out numerous raids on Crimean Tatar cultural and spiritual institutions. On January 27, Russian police raided the Crimean Tatar children's center Elif in Dzhankoi, seizing books and materials. On January 28, police raided the Islamic Cultural Center in Simferopol, again seizing books and materials.

Russian laws imposed on Crimea that regulate NGOs prohibit any group that receives foreign funding and engages in vaguely defined "political activity" to register as a "foreign agent," a term that connotes treason or espionage. While authorities had not included any Crimean NGOs on the list during the year, the law had a chilling effect on their activities (see sections 2.b. and 5 of the *Country Reports on Human Rights* for Russia).

c. Freedom of Religion

See the Department of State's *International Religious Freedom Report* at www.state.gov/religiousfreedomreport/.

d. Freedom of Movement, Internally Displaced Persons, Protection of Refugees, and Stateless Persons

Russian occupation authorities did not respect rights related to freedom of movement and travel.

In-country Movement: There were reports that occupation authorities selectively detained and at times abused persons attempting to enter or leave Crimea. According to human rights groups, Russian authorities routinely detained adult males at the administrative boundary for additional questioning, threatening to seize passports and documents, seizing telephones and memory cards, and questioning them for hours. Crimean residents travelling on Ukrainian passports were required to complete migration paperwork when crossing the administrative boundary between Kherson Oblast and occupied Crimea. As of April 1, Russian authorities forbade Crimean residents with Ukrainian license plates from driving out of Crimea and required all Crimean residents to obtain Russian driver licenses.

On February 25, when Ukrainian journalist Anastasia Ringis attempted to visit her parents in Crimea, Russian authorities prohibited her from entry until 2020. On March 22, Ukrainian authorities reported that Russian occupation authorities banned Kherson residents Rustem Gugurik, Bekir Gugurik, and Bilyal Seytumerov from admission to Crimea for five years.

Occupation authorities also prohibited entry into Crimea by Mustafa Jemilev and Refat Chubarov, members of the Verkhovna Rada and the former and current chairmen of the Crimean Tatar Mejlis, respectively; Crimean Tatar activist Sinaver Kadyrov; and Ismet Yuksel, general director of the Crimean News Agency, on the pretext that they would incite radicalism.

There were reports that authorities forcibly relocated stateless persons in retaliation for their political activism. For example, on November 7, authorities deported Crimean Tatar activist Nedim Khalilov, who had initiated a court case several months earlier against occupation authorities, which sought to have Russia's occupation of Crimea declared illegal. Khalilov possessed only a Soviet identity document, which stated that his place of birth was Uzbekistan. He had obtained neither Ukrainian nor Russian citizenship on ideological grounds. After a brief court hearing, occupation authorities forcibly deported Khalilov to a detention center in Russia; at year's end, he was still awaiting deportation to Uzbekistan, where he had no relatives, housing, or other support.

Citizenship: Russian occupation authorities require all residents of Crimea to be Russian citizens. Those who refuse Russian citizenship may be subjected to arbitrary expulsion. According to the Russian Office of the Federal Bailiff's Service, occupation authorities expelled a couple with Israeli and Ukrainian citizenships from Kerch in February. Additionally, authorities denied those who refused Russian citizenship access to government employment, education, and health care, as well as the ability to open bank accounts and buy insurance, among other limitations. One media report detailed the case of a woman in Yevpatoria who could not have stitches removed because she had not accepted Russian citizenship. In another case, a displaced person from the Donbas could not receive treatment for a dog bite.

According to media sources, Russian authorities prosecuted private employers who continued to employ Ukrainians. According to the Crimea Human Rights Group, on April 8, occupation authorities fined the company Voyazhkrym 35,000 rubles ($570) for employing a Ukrainian. On April 18, authorities fined the Fregat shipbuilding company in Kerch 250,000 rubles ($4,100) for employing a Ukrainian.

In some cases authorities compelled Crimean residents to surrender their Ukrainian passports, complicating international travel, as many countries did not recognize passports issued by Russian occupation authorities.

Occupation authorities announced that, as of January 1, individuals who retained Ukrainian citizenship must register their passports or be subjected to fines or imprisonment.

Internally Displaced Persons

Approximately 30,000 residents of Crimea registered with Ukraine's State Emergency Service as IDPs on the mainland, according to the UN Office for the Coordination of Humanitarian Affairs. The Mejlis and local NGOs, such as Krym

SOS, believed the actual figure could be as high as 100,000 as most IDPs remained unregistered. Many individuals fled out of fear that occupation authorities would target them for abuse because of their work as political activists or journalists. Muslims, Greek Catholics, and Evangelical Christians who left Crimea said they feared discrimination due to their religious beliefs.

Crimean Tatars, who made up the largest number of IDPs, said they were concerned about pressure on their community, including an increasing number of arbitrary searches of their homes, surveillance, and discrimination. Additionally, many professionals left Crimea because Russian occupation authorities required them to apply for Russian professional licenses and adopt Russian procedures in their work.

Section 3. Freedom to Participate in the Political Process

<u>Recent Elections</u>: Russian occupation authorities have prevented residents from voting in Ukrainian national and local elections since Crimea's occupation began in 2014.

On September 18, Russia's nationwide parliamentary elections included seats allocated for occupied Crimea, a move widely condemned by the international community. The Crimea Human Rights Group recorded incidents where occupation authorities coerced residents into voting in the elections, including threats of dismissals and wage cuts.

Section 4. Corruption and Lack of Transparency in Government

<u>Corruption</u>: There were multiple reports during the year of systemic rampant corruption among Crimean "office-holders," including through embezzlement of Russian state funds allocated to support the occupation. According to media reports, more than half of the funding for transportation infrastructure during the year was misspent or unaccounted for, and funds for infrastructure in Crimea were being funneled to the Kerch bridge project without adequate oversight. Human rights sources also reported misspent or stolen medical services funds adversely affected the provision of health care under Russian occupation.

<u>Financial Disclosure</u>: There were no known requirements for Russian occupation authorities or their agents to file, verify, or make public any income or asset disclosure statements, nor was there a mechanism to provide for public access to information about their activities.

Section 5. Governmental Attitude Regarding International and Nongovernmental Investigation of Alleged Violations of Human Rights

Most independent human rights organizations ceased activities in Crimea following Russia's occupation. Occupation authorities refused to cooperate with independent human rights NGOs and ignored their views, and they harassed human rights monitors and threatened them with fines and imprisonment.

Russia continued to deny access to the peninsula to international human rights monitors from the OSCE and the United Nations. A Council of Europe human rights delegation visited Crimea in April.

Section 6. Discrimination, Societal Abuses, and Trafficking in Persons

Children

Birth Registration: Under both Ukrainian law and laws imposed by Russian occupation authorities, either birthplace or parentage determines citizenship. Russia's occupation and purported annexation of Crimea complicated the question of citizenship for children born after February 2014, since it was difficult for parents to register a child as a citizen with Ukrainian authorities. Registration in Ukraine requires a hospital certificate, which is retained when a birth certificate is issued. Under the occupation regime, new parents could only obtain a Russian birth certificate and did not have access to a hospital certificate. During the year Ukrainian government instituted a process whereby births in Crimea could be recognized with documents issued by occupation authorities.

Institutionalized Children: There were reports that Russian authorities continued to permit kidnapping of orphans in Crimea and transporting them across the border into Russia for adoption. Ukraine's government did not know the whereabouts of the children.

Anti-Semitism

According to Jewish groups, an estimated 10-15,000 Jews lived in Crimea, primarily in Simferopol. There were no reports of anti-Semitic acts.

National/Racial/Ethnic Minorities

Since the beginning of Russia's occupation, authorities singled out Crimean Tatars and Ukrainians for discrimination, abuse, deprivation of religious and economic rights, and violence, including killings and abductions (see sections 1.a., 1.b., 1.c., 1.d., 1.f., 2.a., 2.b., and 2.d.).

Crimean Tatars are an ethnic group native to Crimea, dating most recently to the Crimean Khanate of the 15th century. In 1944 Soviet authorities forcibly deported more than 230,000 Crimean Tatars to the Soviet Far East for allegedly collaborating with the Nazis during World War II. Following the dissolution of the Soviet Union, many surviving Crimean Tatars returned to Crimea. Prior to the Russian occupation, there were approximately 300,000 Crimean Tatars living in Crimea.

There were reports that government officials openly advocated discrimination and violence against Crimean Tatars. For example, during a public online discussion on December 13, Natalya Kryzhko, a member of the "parliament," threatened to "load [Crimean Tatars] on barges and drown them in the Black Sea" in reaction to requests by two Crimean Tatar villages to restore their historic Crimean Tatar place names.

Occupation authorities harassed Crimean Tatars for speaking their language in public and forbade speaking it in the workplace. There were reports that teachers prohibited schoolchildren from speaking Crimean Tatar to one another.

Occupation authorities placed restrictions on the Spiritual Administration of Crimean Muslims, which is closely associated with Crimean Tatars. According to human rights groups, Russian security services routinely monitored prayers at mosques for any mention that Crimea remains part of Ukraine. Russian security forces also monitored mosques for anti-Russian sentiment and as a means of recruiting police informants.

Laws forbid religious gatherings outside established institutions. Crimean Tatars reported that Russian occupation authorities threatened the custom of home funeral services and have compiled lists of gravediggers and Muslim leaders.

Russian occupation authorities also targeted ethnic Ukrainians. According to the Crimean Human Rights Group, on June 10, a court convicted Vladimir Baluch of insulting an official during an investigation into a stolen automobile. Baluch maintained the charges were in retaliation for his displays of Ukrainian ethnic symbols and opposition to the occupation. On December 8, the FSB raided

Baluch's home after he posted a sign "renaming" his street in honor of the "heavenly hundred" protesters who died during the 2013-14 Euromaidan protests in Kyiv. During the raid the FSB claimed to have found explosives, which Baluch insists its agents planted, and arrested Baluch. He faced weapons charges carrying a prison term of four years. On December 27, a court extended his detention until February 2017. In 2015 security forces detained and beat Baluch for flying a Ukrainian flag at his home.

Occupation authorities have not permitted churches linked to ethnic Ukrainians, in particular the Ukrainian Orthodox Church-Kyiv Patriarchate (UOC-KP) and the Ukrainian Greek Catholic Church, to register under Russian law. Occupation authorities harassed and intimidated members of the churches and used court proceedings to force the UOC-KP in particular to leave properties it had rented for years. According to a January 16 court decision, the UOC-KP was compelled to vacate part of the St. Vladimir and Olga church in Sevastopol after its lease expired and was required to pay an administrative fine of nearly 600,000 rubles ($9,800). Church officials reported regular and systematic surveillance of UOC-KP churches and parishioners.

Russian occupation authorities targeted businesses and properties belonging to ethnic Ukrainians and Crimean Tatars for expropriation and seizure. Particularly, they prohibited Crimean Tatars affiliated with the Mejlis from registering businesses or properties.

Acts of Violence, Discrimination, and other Abuses Based on Sexual Orientation and Gender Identity

Human rights groups and local gay rights activists reported that much of the LGBTI community fled Crimea after the Russian occupation began. Those who remained live in fear of verbal and physical abuse due to their sexual orientation. According to a report commissioned by the Ukrainian Center for Civil Liberties and Memorial's Antidiscrimination Center in Saint Petersburg, the Russian group Occupy Pedophilia is active in Crimea. The group used social media to lure suspected LGBTI persons to locations where they are humiliated, filmed, and beaten. According to one report, a group of six men patrolling a park beat two individuals in Simferopol. The victims did not file a complaint with police for fear of retaliation. Individuals were accosted and abused for wearing nonconformist clothing, on the assumption that they must be LGBTI persons. Human rights groups stated that these groups operated with the tacit support of local authorities, who did not investigate such crimes.

Russian occupation authorities prohibited any LGBTI groups from holding public events in Crimea. On April 25, an LGBTI activist in Sevastopol announced plans to hold a peaceful protest. In response Sergei Aksyonov, the head of the occupation authorities in Crimea, stated that authorities would prevent any such assembly. Subsequently, "self-defense" forces threatened to expel LGBTI individuals from Crimea forcibly. LGBTI individuals faced increasing restrictions on their right to assemble peacefully, as occupation authorities enforced a Russian law that criminalizes the so-called propaganda of nontraditional sexual relations to minors (see section 6 of the *Country Reports on Human Rights* for Russia).

Section 7. Worker Rights

Russian occupation authorities announced that the labor laws of Ukraine would no longer be in effect after January 1 and that only the laws of the Russian Federation would apply (see section 7 of the *Country Reports on Human Rights* for Russia).

Russian occupation authorities imposed labor laws and regulations of the Russian Federation on Crimean workers, limited worker rights, and created barriers to freedom of association, collective bargaining, and the ability to strike. The NGO Freedom House reported that pro-Russian authorities threatened to nationalize property owned by Ukrainian labor unions in Crimea. Ukrainians who did not accept Russian citizenship faced job discrimination in all sectors of the economy. Only Russian passport holders could continue to work in "government" and municipal positions.